MILAN

History, art, monuments

Published by
ITALCARDS
bologna Italy

Layout
PINUCCIA DE ROSA, CRISTINA MIRABELLI

Photography
PAOLO LIACI

Photo Archives
GIANCARLO COSTA

Edited by
STUDIO DIAKRONIA

Introduction

It is unlikely for someone visiting Milan to remain fascinated by the city as a whole or by some part of it, be it a neighborhood, square, or individual monument. In this brief introduction, in fact, I wish to explicitly invite the visitor not to look for «cheap thrills» and not to attempt hurried decisions. Milan, in spite of its well-appreciated cultural and social abundance, is a city that is difficult to know and to love.

It cannot be said that it is generally ugly, nor that it is openly beautiful, nor can one base a definition on a particular historical era. Its appearance is largely modern, but it is neither convenient nor correct to qualify it as a metropolis which has long sacrificed to the needs of the present most of what links it to the past.

Milan's past is much more ancient and much richer in events than is commonly believed, and is in large part still legible and with sufficient continuity. The present is extremely active, and such that it contains practically all themes, evene the most dramatic, of the era which we are currently living. But, beyond an iconography which is often forcibly aggressive, this does not take anything away from Milan.

It is truly living in equilibrium, perhaps precarious but enviable: on the one hand, the traces of history are not such to oblige us to certain real or metaphorical paths, as occurs, for better or worse, in many Italian cities. On the other hand, the scenarios of the present, here also understood in both the real and metaphorical senses, do not offer themselves in a desolate and disquieting (at least to our sensitivity as citizens of Europe) *tabula rasa*.

What I'd like to say is that this is a city which speaks more to the mind than to the heart: those who wish to hear its voices have to make some effort, not just to seek out the individual historical testimonies, but also to deepen a knowledge which cannot be reached through contemplation alone.

The ideal visitor, to whom this guide is aimed, will be able to reconstruct the history of Milan, not just superficially, and will soon realize how often, from Roman times to today, the city has held a protagonist's role within a context that has often surpassed national boundaries. This is the fundamental reason why each era has left significant monuments, often very important, yet without prevaricating on the others.

This same circumstance lies at the foundation of the clear sensation, which even the most hurried tourist will soon notice, of finding oneself in a place which is open as few others are to a broad-ranging future involving a number of areas, from technology to economics, from science to culture in its various forms of expression.

The signs are so numerous that it is necessary to make drastic selections: it is, in fact, a good idea for someone visiting Milan to emphasize one sector and explore it profoundly, rather than to lose himself in a superficial and disorienting overall review. In this exploration this guide, although deliberately flexible, performs the valuable task of indicating itineraries and sufficient historical information to begin a correct and indepth approach, and of supplying — even to those persons almost exclusively interested in the Milan of today — a foundation of historical knowledge which will certainly not be out of place.

The saying that knowledge of the past is essential in understanding the present holds true for few cities as for Milan. In the salient monuments of the past, the visitor will soon find, as I said, the testimony of the European vocation of the city and its perennial capacity of elaborating, first and better than elsewhere, new ways of life, of behavior, and new economic and cultural models.

Those who visit Milan today should avoid easy stereotypes and the pathetic recollections of a false and often vulgar folklore, to search in the appropriate places, even in the best-known, for the expression of a civilization which has deep and very solid roots, although so difficult to distinguish.

Germano Mulazzani
Superintendence of the Environment
and Monuments of Lombardy

HISTORICAL NOTES

ANCIENT MEDIOLANUM

That the name Milan derives from Mediolanum is certain: more controversial is the origin of the latter, which may be attributed to the ancient Celtic name «Midland», or, according to others, a just as ancient bas-relief representing a sow half covered by wool, from which could be derived «mezzalana» («half-wool»), which could in turn be linked to Mediolanum.

The origins of the first nucleus of Milan are also wrapped in an aura of mystery. According to the historian Tito Livio, the first stone was laid by the chief Gaul, Belloveri, in 603 B.C., and soon the settlement became one of the largest cities of the Transpadano Gauls, who had supplanted the Ligurians. This first nucleus arose on a slight rise in the terrain, located in a vast swampy area, as Milan is on the border between an arid northern area and a southern area rich with forested swamps, where there are now rice fields and irrigated meadows.

It is said that when the Romans conquered the entire area in 222 B.C., they found this large city, located more or less where the Piazza del Duomo was later built, surrounded by a hedge of «andegari», common hawthorn, a denomination which is found in the name of today's via Andegari.

ROMAN MILAN

The Romans began building their own city in the area, but they had to counter with Hannibal and the «Milanese» themselves, his allies. In 169 B.C. the Romans re-conquered Mediolanum and in 49 B.C. Julius Caesar entered with his legions: he greatly appreciated the city for its strategic importance, although, according to tradition, it seems he was disgusted by the butter they used to flavor the asparagus. Caesar raised Milan to a «Municipium», and granted citizenship to its inhabitants. A grandiose theater which seated about 7,000 dates back to this period;

The polygonal tower of Maximilian (III C.A.D.), with its thick walls, the only remainder of the fortified Roman blockade. On the following pages, the 16 Corinthian columns of San Lorenzo and the pre-Christian church of the same name, which represent Milan's Roman past.

its remains are visible beneath the Exchange Building.

The first ring of Roman wall is from the Augustan age and dates to the 1st century A.D. The path corresponds approximately to that of todays via Pattari, via Agnello, via Marino, via Filodrammatici, via Lauro, via Cusani, via San Giovanni sul Muro, via Brisa, via San Sisto, via Stampa, via Cornaggia, via Paolo da Cannobio.

Mediolanum, however, had to wait in order to shine at its brightest, in spite of its growing strategic and commercial importance, until 286 when it was chosen as the residence of the Roman Emperor of the West, Maximilian. He had a grandiose amphitheatre built near what is today via Arena, the Forum near Piazza San Sepolcro and, especially, a new ring of walls which doubled the constructed area from 50 to 100 hectares, and which thus came to include the area which today lies between via Mon-

tenapoleone, Piazza San Babila, corso Europa, the Vegetable Market, Piazza Missori, Piazza Vetra, via Cappuccio, via San Giovanni sul Muro and via Monte di Pietà: in the city, at that time, there lived approximately one hundred thousand people. Of these walls, bearing witness to the past, remain a polygonal tower and a fortified section at the Grand Monastery, and the remains of Porta Ticinensis al Carrobbio. Already some streets were «jammed» by traffic: the main eastern road, via Porticara, corresponding to what is now the beginning of corso di Porta Romana, and along today's via Torino and via Manzoni.

The Roman Milan occupied the area immediately south-west of piazza Duomo, and its SW-SE orientation corresponds to that of today, as it has developed radially from ther original nucleus. The sixteen Corinthian columns in front of the Basilica of San Lorenzo also date back to this period.

important center of Christianity which, according to tradition, was diffused in the city by St. Barnabus in the year 52 AD. A festival is also linked to the legend of St. Barnabus, and is still celebrated today: the flower festival of the «thirteenth of March», which commemorates the miracle of the saint's flowered walking-stick.

It was in Milan that the emperor Constantine proclaimed, in 313, the edict that legalized Christianity and in 391, again from Milan, all non-Christian cults were banned by the emperor Theodosius, strongly influenced by the extremely powerful Milanese bishop Ambrose. Ambrose's thinking in turn reflected that of another great personality of Christianity, Augustine, who had spent a few years of his life in Milan and had been baptized there by Ambrose himself.

CHRISTIAN MILAN

Milan in the meantime had become an

Above, the Chiavalle abbey, founded in 1135 by St. Bernardo di Clairvaux. Next page, the Romanesque church of San Babila (XI cent.).

Christian Milan continued to grow and prosper, escaping in 401 the terrible threat posed by the Visigoth hordes of Alaricus thanks to the military skill of Stilicho. The following year, the emperor Honorius, son of Theodorius, moved the capital of the Roman Empire to Ravenna. Meanwhile, Italy was by now preyed upon by the barbarian hordes, who also fell upon Milan: in 452, Attila's Huns, who did however spare the city thanks to the words of its bishop; in 489 the Ostrogoths of Theodoric; in 538 the Goths and Burgundians, who massacred tens of thousands of citizens and deported children and women; and finally, the Longobards of Alboin, who entered Milan in 569 and gave the region its name, which has lasted until today.

These were not flourishing times for the metropolis, which saw its own predomination strongly contrasted by Pavia and Castelseprio, and its power weakened by the partitioning done by the Longobard king Agilulfo, who assigned Pavia to one son, Godeberto, and Milan to the other, Bertarido. In any case, it appears that during the Longobard period Milan already had eight gates. But for the city to re-acquire its earlier prestige it had to wait for Charlemagne, who favored Milan and Pavia and also chose Milan as the seat of a mint. During the chaos following the death of Charlemagne, among the domination at times Byzantine, at times Longobard, the bishops took on great importance, with special note for Ariberto d'Intimiano, in 1018 consecrated archbishop of Milan.

Ariberto, more a prince than a man of the church, consecrated Conrad II as emperor and asked for his help in combatting the vavasors, vassals of the archbishop, who had rebelled against him and whom he had been unable to defeat during the battle of Campomalo (1136).

The alliance between Conrad and Ariberto was not destined to last long: Conrad was chased out by the Milanese, but later reinforced his power and imprisoned Ariberto, who did not intend to renounce his role as spokesman for the Ambrosian church. Ariberto managed to escape, and elected himself chief of the Milanese united against Conrad.

MILAN THE CITY-STATE

The emperor, however, was able to deprove the archbishop of his power with the *Constitutio de Feudis* (May 1037), which established the equality of vavasors and the rich feudal lords before the law, not even the death of Conrad II, in 1039, was sufficient to return peace to Milan, where the new class of *burgenses* — bankers, landowners and merchants — basically the emerging and supporting force of the Milanese economy, requested greater participation in running the city, guided by Lanzone. Peace returned with the emperor Henry III, who threatened to send 4,000 horsemen to attack Milan.

In the period following the death of Ariberto, in 1045, Milan was tormented by a continuously changing society, a corrupt and simoniacal curia under the aegis of the archbishop Guido da Velate and a generally poor government which prepared the terrain for the «pataria», a popular movement headed by Landolfo and Erlembardo Colta which asked for the church's return to original poverty. The pataria succeeded in chasing the corrupt archbishop from Milan and in making converts until the death of Erlembardo in 1075.

The feats of the priest Liprando, a singer of popular tradition, fall into this context. The Patarines were then abandoned by those who had once supported them, who accepted the plan for reform proposed by the archbishop Anselmo da Bovisio.

From the collaboration between the archbishop and the high bourgeoisie, a new system of communal government was born and consolidated. The community is subject to the power of the archbishop, but follows its own objectives, mainly that of opening new ways to facilitate commerce, an activity which is taking on increasing proportions. This need to open new means of communication leads, in 1111, to the conquest and destruction of Lodi, an important passage to the Po Valley, and to the taking of Como in 1127, with the consequent control of the Lugano and Chiasso passes, both also of fundamental importance for commerce.

Federico Barbarossa (Redbeard) is the one who stops the expansion of Milan: a first siege in 1158 ends with the promise by the Milanese not to oppose the reconstruction of Lodi and Como, while the second siege in 1161 has the disastrous result of destroying the city, made still more catastrophic and ferocious by the revenge of the other Lombard cities, who in the past had been forced to bear its hegemony. In an attempt to oppose the sieges by Barbarossa, the Milanese had dug a circular trough, approximately four hundred meters from the exterior of the Maximilian walls, by now inadequate, using the earth extracted to erect a belt of bastions (*terragium*) on the path of what is today known as the «cerchia de navigli». For four years the citizens were forced to live camped outside the walls, but they found the strength to resurge and, under the banner of the Lombard League, defeated Barbarossa in the battle of Legnano on 29 May 1176. The peace of Costanza of 1183 sanctioned the right of the Milanese to elect their counsels without the interference of the archbishop and the legal recognition of the Milanese consolate, although still dependent on the emperor.

The Archbishop's palace in piazza del Duomo. Built in 1170 on the episcopal area destroyed by Barbarossa, it was expanded in the XV century.

MILAN OF THE VISCONTIS AND SFORZAS

Many important testimonies in the field of architecture remain from the centuries of the High Middle Ages: the apsidal part of Sant'Ambrogio, from the 8th century, the apse of San Vincenzo in Prato, the sacellum of San Satiro, the churches of Sant'Eustorgio, San Babila, San Celso, San Nazaro Maggiore and San Simpliciano, all from the 4th century.

The events following the peace of Constance see the Milanese involved in negotiations with their neighbors, and especially with Lodi, Vercelli, Como, to ensure their commercial expansion. The struggles with the emperor were over, but the new bourgeois class, the economic force of the city, pushed to gain greater power. In 1109 they create the Credence of Sant'Ambrogio against the traditional and aristocaratic *comune militum*. In 1216 the institution of a regular podesta government is recorded, which ensures all citizens of legal equality. In this period, Milan has approximately 90,000 inhabitants. The wool and metal industries flourish, while commerce receives a big push from the shipbuilding industry.

The commercial interests lead the way to the struggles which will make Milan move from the Torriani government to that of the Viscontis, and then to the Sforzas. Martino della Torre ingratiates popular opinion with important public works and succeeds in procuring enormous powers for his brother Filippo as well.

The domination of the Torrianis is replaced by that of the Viscontis: after nearly eighty year of struggle between the two families, in 1311 the Torrianis are finally eliminated from the political scene. The ferocity practiced on the Torriani residence is remembered today in the same of one of the city's streets: via Case Rotte («Broken Houses»). The Visconti dynasty lasted one hundred and thirty-six years: after Matteo, grandson of the first Archbishop Ottone, Azzone Visconti beautified Milan, paving the streets with stones laid in a fish-bone pattern, restoring

and finishing those walls begun as a defence against Barbarossa, reinforcing the gates and decorating them with the snake of the Visconti coat-of-arms, expanding the fortifications at Porta Ticinese so that they also included Sant'Eustorgio, where the Visconti tombs are located, completing the churches of Sant'Eustorgio, San Simpliciano and San Marco. Gian Galeazzo Visconti received the title of duke in 1395, when costruction had already begun on the Duomo (1383).

With Filippo Maria Visconti, who relieved the population of the military burdens entrusted to the soldiers of fortune, a new boom was recorded in commerce and agriculture, in which rice and mulberry cultivation were introduced, useful to the new silk industry.

The death of Filippo Maria in 1447, with no heirs, openend the way to Francesco Sforza, whose dynasty will rule until 1535. These are years of great intellectual and artistic fervor, which give birth to magnificent works: the Univesity, are built, and some of the greatest artistic geniuses of all time are active in Milan: Leonardo da Vinci and Bramante.

SPANISH AND AUSTRIAN MILAN

Having reached the peak of glory and prosperity, Milan and its duchy passed through dark centuries after the last of the Sforzas, Francesco II, was expelled. These are the years of Spanish domination. Burdened by taxes and levies on every kind of merchandise and goods, racked by two plague epidemics in 1576 and in 1630, the last spendidly described in Manzoni's *The*

Here, the statue of St. George with the facial features of Gian Galeazzo Visconti, preserved in the Duomo Museum. Facing page, a tower of the Sforza Castle.

Betrothed, the Milanese arrive at the *historic minimum*, in spite of the political and cultural dedication of the cardinal Federico Borromeo, cousin of Carlo Borromeo who finances and oversees the building of the Library (1609) and the Ambrosian Art Gallery (1621). Among the few architectural works of this period, the most notable are the Brera courtyard, and the Litta and Cusani Palaces, while in the painting field the sumptuous fresco by Tiepolo in Palazzo Clerici is significant; but all of this is not sufficient to erase the image of a poor and dirty city, which spreads out in a labyrinth of smelly alleyways, the home of markets of every type and of brigandage, lined with shrouded windows, filthy rags placed to cover the openings.

These are the occurrences and recurrences of history, mother and stepmother. They must wait for other foreigners, namely the Austrians, in the person of the Empress Maria Theresa who rises to the throne in 1740, for their economic and social comeback. Maria Theresa, who considered Lombardy to be one of her most potentially profitable properties, launched important reforms which caused commerce and industry to flourish, intensified the struggle against bandits, removed suffocating taxes and duties, introduced protective levies and most of all gave the order to start work on the draft of the land register, which went into effect in 1760.

In Milan and its surroundings, industries of all kinds arise: glass works, paper mills, spinning mills, silk and wool weavers; the streets, which will be catalogued in 1787 with the new toponymy assigning a number to each house, are paved; as early as 1775, the «window shrouds» were nearly all replaced by glass panes. Milan counted approximately 126.000 inhabitants, of which 93,000 were peasants, 21,000 bourgeoisie, 6,700 clerical and 5,600 nobles. Culture undergoes a strong resurgence, with personages such as L.A. Muratori, Verri, Parini, Beccaria, and the intellectuals who bring illuministic culture, as well as art and architecture, to Milan. Giuseppe Piermarini is the father of one of the symbols of Milan, the La Scala Theatre, inaugurated amidst general acclaim in 1778 with «L'Europa riconosciuta» by Salieri. Another symbol of Milan dates to 1774: the «Madonnina» on the highest spire of the Duomo.

RISORGIMENTO
AND MODERN MILAN

In 1796 Napoleon entered Milan and on July 9, 1797 the city was chosen as the capitol of the Cisalpine Republic. Although independence was far away, Milan continued to expand, prosper, and create culture with La Scala, which was all the rage with the staging of operas by Mozart and Rossini, and with Ugo Foscolo who wrote hymns to the fatherland and seduced girls of all ages. The streets were no longer the accomplices of lovers and assassins, as the street illumination had been perfected. New and elegant streets were also opened, such as via Moscova, the Public Gardens and the by-pass between Porta Romana and Porta Marengo (Ticinese) and Porta Orientale (Venezia) were organized and the Arena was completed. In many streets, however, the patrician buildings contrasted sharply with the many shacks of the poor, who were magnanimously assisted by works of charity.

The general discontent gained ground, especially due to the economic inequality and the obligatory draft, which had paid too high a tribute in blood. The minister of finance, Giuseppe Prina, was lynched by the crowd on April 20, 1814, the French left the city and Radetszky arrived. In the past, Austrian domination had contributed to the city's prosperity, but by now the Milanese were politicalized to the right degree and many joined the revolutionary movements of 1821. Radetzky reacted by striking hard, especially against the Carbonari and the Confederates and sending many to prison, such as Maroncelli who ended up at the Spielberg along with Silvio Pellico.

But the Milanese did not bow their heads: smoking strikes, eating watermelon (red, white and green..) under the nose of the invader, and more concrete manifestations led to March 18, 1848, the «cinque giornate» (5 days) during which the people in revolt chased out the Austrians. It was a brief victory, the Austrians would return and remain until the Second War of Independence, but by then Milan was ready to be only Italian, once again aiming towards economic and social development.

Above left, the church of San Fedele, erected by order of St. Carlo Borromeo in 1569.
Facing page, top, the neoclassical façade of the Palazzo Reale, by Piermarini; bottom, the church of San Marco, whose façade was rebuilt in 1871 in a catching Gothic-Lombard style.

In 1864 the Railway Station was inaugurated; in 1873 the suburbs known ad «Corpi Santi» (Holy Bodies) were engulfed, in 1876 the newspaper «Corriere della Sera» was born, and in 1880 the «Magazzini Bocconi», which later became «La Rinascente», were opened.

Politically, socially and economically, in the following years Milan was the undisputed fulcrum of the development of Italy. The railway system was expanded and banks and industries sprouted. The first socialist movements, in which were involved among others personages such as Filippo Turati and Anna Kuliscioff, found an extremely fertile terrain in the city's proletariat, which especially in 1898 will have to pay a bloody price under the cannons and guns of Bava Beccaris.

The interventionist movement, futurism, and the Scapigliatura movement originate in Milan, which in 1922 also sees the birth of the Fascist party. The following year a number of surrounding communities are aggregated to the city of Milan, in this way

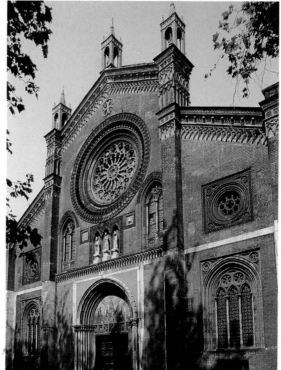

inevitably losing their rural town character, with its predominantly agricultural economy, to become city suburbs.

In the 1931 census, the metropolitan territory covered 18,883 hectares, against the 7,396 of the 1901 census, and Milan arrived at one million inhabitants.

In the years of Fascism, the urban structure of the city changes: the Canal is partially covered, Piazza San Babila is gutted to make room for corso del Littorio, now corso Matteotti. The new Central Railway Station is inaugurated, and the Exchange Building, the Niguarda Main Hospital and the Hydroport are built. In '42 and in August of '43, Milan is nearly razed to the ground by bombings: 80 per cent of the city buildings were damaged. The historic center, with La Scala, the Galleria and corso Vittorio Emanuele was a pile of ruins: the electrical, gas, and water conduits were ruined, schools and public buildings were destroyed, and the factories, including Pirelli, Breda, and Alfa Romeo, were damaged.

After the war, the Milanese roll up their sleeves and the city's reconstruction begins. La Scala, which had been completely destroyed,

is newly inaugurated in 1946, the new historic center rises up, private houses, public buildings, and stores are rebuiet. In 1955, the Pirelli skyscraper challenger the height of the Madonnina, and in the Seventies the subway becomes practically the symbol of the frenetic pace of the Milanese as they head towards progress and an unstoppable cult of efficiency.

Above, the Duomo; facing page, the Pirelli skyscraper, two symbols of ancient and modern Milan.

ITINERARY Nr.1:
THE HISTORICAL NUCLEUS

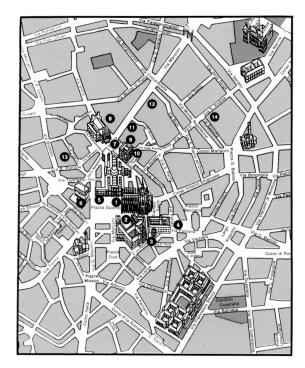

DUOMO

The square in front of the Duomo was built, after the Unification of Italy, in an area previously occupied by the Rebecchino district and the Coperto dei Figini. The square is currently closed to the west by the Advertising Building, to the south by the southern porticos and the Communal Palace, to the north by the northern porticos with the Galleria and to the east by the Duomo. In Roman times a temple, probably dedicated to Minerva, stood at the point where the Duomo was erected. Halfway through the IV century, Ambrose had basilica built over what is now the church courtyard, known as Nova et Maior to differentiate it from a pre-existing holy construction known as Vetus et Minor, of which no traces remain. In the Basilica Nova was the baptistry of San Giovanni alle Fonti, where Ambrose baptized Augustine in 387.

In the VII century, the basilica was entitled Santa Tecla, and in 836 another was built and named Santa Maria Maggiore, where sacred rites where held during the winter, while summer rites continued to be celebrated in the first. Santa Tecla was destroyed in 1075, together with an ex-

tremely rich library, by a terrible fire. It was then demolished in the mid-XV century because construction had begun in the meantime on the current Duomo, which takes its name from Domus

Two views of the Domo with the Madonnina and the slender gothic spires.

Sanctii Ambrosii, house of Saint Ambrose, which was located on the area of what is today the Archbishop's Palace.

It was Gian Galeazzo Visconti who began the construction in 1386, preparing the Candoglia marble quarries on Lake Maggiore. The huge blocks of marble were transported to Milan by barges which navigated on the Ticino River and then on the Grand Canal, and were unloaded into a dockyard similar to a pond, which is remembered today in via Laghetto (Pond Street).

The marble destined for the Duomo bore the initials AUF (*Ad usum fabricae*) to indicate that they were exempt from duty. For this reason the expression came into common use to indicate work for no compensation, free of charge, and gradually became «a *ufo*».

The Duomo, as can be admired today, is the work of a thousand hands, which fits into the tradition of Gothic cathedrals: architects and engineers from many countries took part in it, especially Germans. It was however Napoleon who gave it its definitive look when he had the façade built.

This basilical church, the third-largest in the world after St. Peter's at the Vatican and the Cathedral of Seville, can host 40,000 people in its 12,000 square meters. The width from one end of the transept to the other is 92 meters, and it is 157 meters long; the highest spire is 109 meters tall, and in 1774 the golden statue of the Madonna was placed upon it. 145 spires soar into the sky, and the exterior is decorated with 2,245 statues, 96 «giant» gargoyles and a large number of half-figures sculpted into the window frames. 500 steps lead to the terrace of the main spire, 261 to the lantern and 158 to the roof, where one can also arrive via a modern elevator. The best point for observing the beautiful apsidal complex is the beginning of the Galleria Vittorio Emanuele II.

The celebrated Milanese architect Francesco Maria Richini began the façade at the beginning of the XVII century, and the work was not completed — after much controversy — until 1812. The lower part of the work is in Baroque style, while the upper part is more Gothic. The base is enriched with 52 bas-reliefs, the work of 17th-century Baroque sculptors, depicting *Scenes from the Old Testament*. Five majestic portals with large windows above them break up the façade, first with triangular tympanums and then, moving upwards, Gothic styling, decorated with

A glimpse of the upper part of the Duomo's façade and the detail of a rose window.

sculptureal altorilievos after a design by Cerano (early XVII century).

The bronze doors which close the portals represent, from the right: the *Glories of the Duomo to the time of St. Charles* by Luciano Minguzzi (1965), the *Events in Milan from the destruction of Barbarossa to the vistory at Legnano by* Franco Lombardi (1942) and Virginio Pessina (1950), *History life of St. Ambrose* by Giannino Castiglioni (1950), *Constantine's Edict* by Arrigo Minerbi (1840).

On the sides of the Duomo, high windows and buttresses alternate and then converge at the pillars of the nave in flying buttresses. All of it is embellished with marble decorations: one example is the beautifull polygonal apse onto which open three large marble-veined windows, a work by Filippo degli Organi in the early XV century. Imposing statuary works grace the sides and the apse.

From the terrace paved with slightly inclined slabs of marble, which can be reached by climbing 919 steps or by elevator, on a clear day one can admire the Lombard Alps and the entire panorama of Milan. A grandiose spectacle is also offered by the expanse of spires and statues, the oldest of which is the Carelli spire, guarded over by the statue of St. George (which has the facial features of Gian Galeazzo Visconti), located in the far corner near corso Vittorio Emanuele. The octagonal lantern is also admirable, the work of Giovanni Antonio Amedeo (1447-1522), based on a design for which Bramante and Leonardo da Vinci were also consulted.

Inside, the Latin cross layout of the building has five longitudinal naves and three on the tranept, divided by 52 huge pillars, topped by capitals with statues in the niches.

Right nave. Starting from the entrance, one finds the sarcophagus of the Archbishop Ariberto d'Intimiano and the copy of the thirteenth-century crucifix of Ariberto, the original of which is kept in the Duomo Museum, which could be that of the city Carroccio, designed by the same archbishop in the period of struggle between the City and Federico Barbarossa. Next we find the stone commemorating the foundation of the Duomo in 1386, the sarcophagus of Ottove Visconti, the sarcophagus of Marco Carelli by Filippo degli Organi, the Brentano stone with a never-realized design for the façade of the Duomo (1866) and the sepulchre of the canon Vimercati, by Bambaia (1546). The three 16th century altars which follow are by Pellegrini. The beautiful window, in which is found what is left of the *Stories of the New Testament*, dates back to 1424, and was part of the apsidal window.

Right Transept. Here we find the tomb of Gian Giacomo Medici, from 1563, and his statue in the central shrine, the statue of the flaying of St. Bartholomew, and a beautiful 16th-century window with some still older panes (1400).

Presbytery. It was begun by Tibaldi in 1567, and it was later raised by the same artist according to the wishes of Carlo Borromeo; Tibaldi also designed the main altar and the wooden chancel. At the top of the vault of the apse we find the radial-cross tabernacle, where since 1461 there has been the Holy Nail of the Cross, which according to tradition the empress Helena gave to her son Constantine and then recovered by St. Ambrose. A marble staircase leads down to the magnificent early Christian altar of the ancient basilica of Santa Tecla.

The ambulatory surrounds the entire presbytery, and here we find the beautiful door of

the southern sacristy dating from 1393. Built into the adjacent wall, the monument to Pope Martin V by Jacopino da Tradate (1424), and in front of it the entrance to the "scurolo" of St. Charles, an underground octagonal chapel by Richini in 1606, where the saint's body is preserved in a silver and rock crystal urn.

Nearby we find the prestigious Treasure of the Duomo, a splendid collection of high liturgical craftsmanship. Still in the ambulatory, the door to the northern sacristy, sculpted in 1389, beyond which traces of the Lombard-Romanesque style can be found, which preceded the Gothic style. The entire ambulatory is lit by three grandiose

On the facing page, one of the Duomo's five bronze portals. Above, some of the sculptures which decorate the exterior of the cathedral. Here, a bas-relief located over the entrance to one of the two sacristies.

windows dating from the sixteenth century.

Left transept. Here the enormous Trivulzio Candelabra, also known as the tree, is hosted: five meters long, made of bronze, it is the work of XII-century French goldsmiths. In front, the tombstone of Federico Borromeo and, in the back, the chapel of the Madonna dell'Albero by Richini. Here the most ancient and original altar is also found, from the year 1300. Nicolò da Varallo is the artist of the beautiful window on the right, which represents *Stories of St. John of Damascus* (1479).

Left nave. On the last of the three altars by Pellegrini there is a wooden crucifix carried in precession by St. Charles during the plague of 1576. Further towards the exit, the Renaissance Mausoleum by Galeazzo Alessi and Cristoforo Lombardi (XVI century), where three arch-

On these pages, some details of the Duomo's interior: top to bottom, a window and bas-reliefs, sarcophagus of Pellegrini, organ, an altar and bas-reliefs above the sacristies. On the following pages, other details of the interior.

27

bishops of the Arcimboldi family are buried. Immediately following, two sheets of marble from the demolished church of Santa Maria Maggiore, with eight apostolic figures. The Baptistry was designed by Pellegrini and the baptismal font is a late Imperial Roman urn.

From a staircase in the counter-façade one descends four meters below the level of the square and arrives at the what was floor level in the IV century, where interesting Roman artifacts may be found such as the foundation of Santa Tecla and the drawing of the Baptistry of San Giovanni alle Fonti, the most ancient example of an octagonal Christian baptistry. Its perimeter, reproduced in marble tiles, is visible at the threshold of the Duomo.

DUOMO MUSEUM

Located in the Royal Palace, opposite the south side of the Duomo, since 1853 it has gathered quite a lot of documentary material and numerous works of art, especially sculptures, which were once part of the Duomo complex, in order to prevent smog and exposure to the open air form deteriorating them further. Perfect copies replace these works in their original position.

The first of these works can be seen at the entrance: it is a head of the Holy Father in copper and gold, designed by Jacopino da Tradate, which was once used as a keystone cover in the absidal semi-dome of the Duomo. In ROOM II, the original of the statue of St. George resembling Gian Galeazzo Visconti, which reigned on the Carelli spire, can be seen next to a block of Candoglia marble. Further on, two "anthelions" can be seen which were part of the oldest window of the Duomo.

In ROOM III are numerous works from the Visconti period, statues from the outside of the

Above, the interior of a room of Duomo Museum.
On the facing page, top, the head of the Holy Father in copper and gold, designed by Jacopino da Tradate; below, the Madonna with child and angels of the 14th century.

Duomo, pillar capitals, original gargoyles and two casts of the giants. To note among the statues, *San Babila and the three girls*, by Matteo Raverti (1404), an example of Lombard Gothic art form which the stylistic differences with respect to transalpine art of the same period can be seen.

In ROOM VI, the fragment of a canvas by Cerano, *The miracle of the woman in labor*; in number VII, the *Crucifix of Ariberto* (1040) and the *Madonna with child and two angels*, a work of the Rhine school from the late 1300's; in number XIII, the original iron supporting structure of the Madonna from 1772, now replaced by stainless steel. ROOM XV holds the designs for the façade of the Duomo, ROOM XVI hosts the

great wooden projection of the Duomo, begun in 1519 and finished towards the end of the 19th century with a design by Brentano for the façade which was never realized.

In the last two rooms is gathered the material documenting the great static restoration of the lantern pillars of the Duomo, carried out by Passano under the guidance of the first architect of Ferrari Duomo Construction between 1981 and 1985.

Visiting hours: 9:30 a.m. - 12:30 p.m./3-6 p.m
Closed Mondays except on holidays.

view of the Royal Palace and a glimpse of the Duomo.

ROYAL PALACE

The first nucleus of what is to become the current Royal Palace dates back to the XI century. Then it was a quadrilateral building, known as the Old Town Hall, the first seat of the Milan City-State, then the residence of the Torriani and Visconti families. Azzone Visconti completed the expansion work begun by his forefathers, adding in 1334 a large arcaded court with ten arcades per side and four towers at the corners: the remains can be seen on the wall of the building at nr. 3 of via Restelli.

The interior decorations were assigned to Giovanni di Balduccio of Pisa and probably to Giotto. After the assassination of Giovanni Ma-

33

ria Visconti in 1412, the Visconti residence was moved to the castle which will later be named after the Sforzas, and which at that time was newly built.

The antique Visconti residence was destroyed during the Ambrosian Republic, and rebuilt by order of Francesco Sforza, who had the side in front of the Duomo shortened as it interfered with the work. When Sforza moved to the Sforza Castle, the palace fell into disrepair, later becoming the seat of the Spanish rulers and undergoing a poorly balanced Baroque transformation.

The architect Giuseppe Piermarini, under the Austrian government, had the side facing the Duomo removed, thereby creating what is now piazzetta Reale. The building was called the Royal Ducal Palace, then the National Palace during the Cisalpine Republic, the Royal Court under Napoleon and then the Royal Palace after the Unification of Italy. In 1902, Vittorio Emanuele granted it to the City of Milan. It now hosts the Superintendence of Monuments of Lombardy, the Museum of Contemporary Art, spaces for various exhibits and shows and the Duomo Museum.

The façade, by Piermarini, has two lateral extensions. The windows of the ground floor have flat tympanums, those of the *piano nobile*, dat-

ing from the 1600's, have alternating triangular and curved tympanums. In order to reach the interior one enters a court of honor, then another courtyard which flows into a third, opening into via Pecorari. The staircase of honor begins in the latter and leads to the splendid interior rooms decorated by famous artists such as Martino Knoller and Francesco Hayez. These halls were heavily damaged by bombing during the last world war.

The CIVIC MUSEUM OF CONTEMPORARY ART has been housed in the Royal Palace only since 1984. Its goal is to represent contemporary works, and with this aim hosts research laboratories open to new orientations an continually changing exhibitions. Numerous works by the most succesful contemporary artists are on display, including Boccioni, De Chirico, Fontana, Martini, Melotti, Morandi, Sironi.

Hours: 9:30 a.m. - 12:15 p.m. / 2:30-5:15 p.m. *Closed Mondays*.

COMMUNAL PALACE

Made up of two marble-covered pavilions, it base has large portals. It was begun in 1939 and finished in 1956.

The pavilion near the southern porticos host the communal offices and the offices of a zoning committee, while the one looking out over piazzetta Reale is the headquarters of the Provincial Tourism Association and occasionally host exhibits and other shows.

CHURCH OF SAN GOTTARDO IN CORTE

Built according to the wishes of Azzone Visconti in 1336, it saw Giovanni Maria Visconti fall victim to a conspiracy before its door in 1412. It belonged to the Visconti Palace as the ducal chapel, and its entrance is now in via Pecorari.

The church boasts one of the most beautiful bell towers of the city, the work of Francesco Pecorari of Cremona, an example of the Lombard Roman style in its round and pointed arches.

Inside, the neoclassical interventions of Piermarini and the later post-war restorations cause the disappearance of most of the original structure. The fresco of the *Crucifixion* of the Gothic school and the remains of the funeral monument of Azzone Visconti, attributed to Giovanni di Balduccio of Pisa, are significant.

ARCHBISHOP'S PALACE

Constructed around 1170 on the site of the ancient archbishop's palace, destroyed by Barbarossa, it was then expanded and changed by the bishops of the Arcimboldi family in the late 1400's. Other interventions were ordered from Pellegrini by Carlo Borromeo in 1570; the cardinal Filippo Visconti later assigned the restructuring to Piermarini. It is separeted from the Royal Palace by via Arcivescovado.

The elegant neoclassical front is broken by two kinds of windows: flat tympanums at the ground floor, triangular tympanums at the secondo floor. The 16th-century portal opens onto Piazza Fontana.

The side facing the Duomo has had the 18th-century façade removed, and now the original brickwork stands out, allowing the various stratifications from over the centuries to be seen. It is still the seat of the Archbishopry.

The interior includes two beautiful curtyards. The smallest, known as Arcimboldo, is entered from Piazza Fontana and contains two 17th-century statues depicting St. Ambrose and St. Charles; the other courtyard, known as the Canonica, is considered Pellegrini's masterpiece. he was however unable to complete the works, which ended in 1604, eight years after his death. Surrounded by a rectangular, two-storey quadriportico, it is dominated by the statues of *Moses*, by Tantardini, and *Aaron*, by Strazza, both from the 1800's.

The Pilgrims' Rotunda, an appendix of the Archbishopry and facing via delle Ore, hosted the stalls for the clergymen's horses on its three floors unitl the eighteenth century.

Facing page, the XVI-century portal of the Archbishop's Palace. Right, the lovely bell tower of the church of St. Gottardo in Corte.

GALLERIA VITTORIO EMANUELE II

It interrupts the northern porticos of the piazza Duomo and connects it to piazza della Scala.

Construction of the Galleria was begun in 1865 after a design by Giuseppe Mengoni, inaugurated in 1897 by the sovereing after whom it is named, and enriched the following year by the triumphal Arch towards piazza del Duomo. It was one of the first iron and glass structures, and today is one of the most elegant covered streets in the country.

The layout is a Latin cross, with the longer

Three enchanting views of the Galleria Vittorio Emanuele II.

arm measuring 196 meters in length, 14.5 meters in width and 32 meters tall, while the crossarm is 105 meters long.

The wide central cupola is 39 meters in diameter and is 47 meters high. Below, mosaics placed in four large lunettes represent Europe, Asia, Africa and America. The cupola rests over the Octagon of the Galleria, at one time decorated with stucco-works.

The Galleria is completely lined with elegant boutiques, prestigious bookstores and card shops, cafés and restaurants. The "Camparino", furnished by Eugenio Quarti and with mosaics by Angelo D'Andrea, is located to the left of the triumphal arch, while the "Motta" is to the right; proceeding on that side there is the famous restaurant "Savini" and the "Biffi".

PIAZZA DEI MERCANTI

To the left of the Galleria, at the north-west corner of the piazza del Duomo, we find the lovely medieval square which was once lined with the main public buildings during the City-State period. It is now bordered by the street of the same

Piazza dei Mercanti with its XVI-century well and the statue of Oldrado da Tresseno on horseback in the Palazzo della Ragione.

name and via Orefici. At one time it was called New Town Hall, and Piazza dei Mercanti was bordered by Palazzo della Ragione and Palazzo dei Giureconsulti to the north.

The six gates which broke up the square are recognizable today in the passage to the Palatine Schools which leads to via Orefici, the ancient gate of San Michele al Gallo, in the Passaggio degli Osii, the ancient Prison gate, again linked to via Orefici, in the passage to piazza del Duomo, the ancient vault of the old Fish Market, in the opening towards Porta Romana, ancient gate to the Podestà, in the Santa Margherita Passage, and in the connection with piazza Cordusion, the old vault of the Fustagnari family.

At the center of the square is the well, until 1879 situated where via Mercanti passes today, built from a sixteenth-century well curb known as the "stone of failure", topped by two Ionic columns holding a triangular tympanum.

PALAZZO DELLA RAGIONE

Constructed according to orders by the Oldrado da Tresseno podesta in 1228, it was also called New Town Hall because it replaced the Old Town Hall located in what is now piazzetta reale. The name "broletto, brolo" in the High Middle Ages referred to the field in which the archbishop exercised justice in the period following the end of Longobard power. It was the home of the community offices until 1786. The Austrians had an additional floor built to house the notary Archives. It is the most interesting example of a Lombard medieval public building and borders piazza dei Mercanti to the north, towards the street of the same name.

The lower external part includes a vast porticoed area with fully rounded arches and ogives at the ends. On the side facing the square, a Romanesque alto-rilievo, the most antique equestrian sculpture known from the Middle Ages, represents Oldrado da Tresseno. The second floor is adorned by large three-light windows and the added floor built under Maria Theresa of Austria has roundels. If one observes the building from via Mercanti, near the second arch from the left one can see the ancient sculpture of the "Half-wooled ewe", or "mezza lana", from which some believe the name Mediolanum derives.

Inside there is an enormous hall, known as the "Sala della Ragione".

PIAZZA DELLA SCALA

One enters by crossing the Gallery along the main axis. The square as it appears today was built in 1859-60 in an area previously covered by buildings. It is the work of the architect Luca Berltrami, who not only completed the façade of Palazzo Marino but also designed the buildings of the Banca Commerciale Italiana which border it.

In the center, the monument to Leonardo da Vinci, created in 1872 by the architect Pietro Magni, surround by statues of this favorite students: Marco d'Oggiono, Cesare da Sesto, Andrea Solaino and Giovanni Antonio Boltraffio.

LA SCALA THEATRE

The first stone of the world's most famous opera theatre was laid in 1776, the year in which the ancient court theatre of the Royal Palace was destroyed in a fire. The location was that of the church of Santa Maria alla Scala, built in 1381 under the direction of Beatrice Regina della Scala, wife of Barnabò Visconti. Designed by the omnipresent Piermarini, the theatre was inaugurated on August 3rd 1778 with Antonio Salieri's opera *L'Europa riconosciuta*. Destroyed by bombings, it was immediately reconstructed and re-inaugurated on May 11, 1946 by the great

Toscanini, who directed a symphony concert there. In via Filodrammatici, next to La Scala, there is the entrance to the "Piccola Scala" where ballets and concerts are held and new voices area introduced.

Neoclassical in style, a central portion of the front is projected forward and preceded by a portico with three arcades. The terraces above date from 1860. On the second floor, double columns and Corinthian pilasters flank the windows with triangular tympanums. On the top floor, the neoclassical bas-relief *Apollo's carriage being chased by the night* is framed by a pediment.

The foyer is decorated with marble and mirrors. The hall was originally decorated with Baroque paintings, followed by neoclassical-style decorations and finally with those we see today, which date to 1830 and are the work of the scenographer Alessandro Sanquirico. The current decorations of the vault are from the same year. The horseshoe-shaped hall has four sets of seats and two galleries, and overall has four up to 3,000 people. Up to 800 actors can move on the 780 square meters of stage, including the backstage area, flanked by Corinthian columns. The splendid bohemian chandelier, dating from 1923, is lit by 365 light bulbs.

Calaf senza mantello

·6·

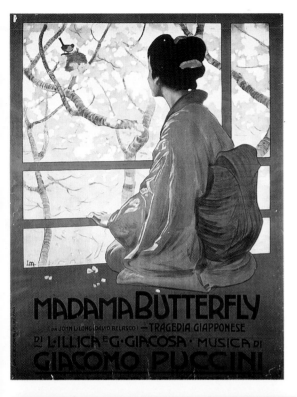

THEATRE MUSEUM

Reached from the theatre, under the left portico of the atrium. Founded in 1911, it gathers together souvenirs and curios regarding the theatre. It is divided into 14 rooms: number I recounts the events of La Scala and the previous theatres and contains busts of musicians; in number II is displayed, among other things, a painting showing the façade of La Scala; number III gathers busts of famous musicians, number IV and V interesting examples of Greek and Roman theatre. Rooms VI and VII hold the Verdi Collection. On the upper floor, room VIII contains musical instruments, room IX busts of artists, including Eleonora Duse, room X is dedicated to the *commedia dell'arte*, room XI more antique musical instruments, in XII and XIII theatre costumes are displayed, and in the last are documents of Oriental theatre.

On the facing page, top, the La Scala Theatre; bottom, a costume of Turandot, preserved at the Theatre Museum. This page, above, poster of the first production of Madame Butterfly and, below, the script of Ciro in Babilon by Rossini (1818) at the Theatre Museum.

PALAZZO MARINO

Located between Piazza San Fedele and Piazza della Scala, it was built in 1558 according to the wishes of the wealthy tax collector Tomaso Marino, who hired Galeazzo Alessi for the occasion. It was a long and difficult task: the honor staircase was finished in 1600, the façade nearest La Scala had to wait instead until 1889 to be completed by the architect Luca Beltrami, who modelled it after the others. In the 1700's it hosted the duty offices. Since 1860 it is the property of the City of Milan, who has made it the seat of the Municipality. It was rebuilt after the Second World War for the damages incurred during bombings.

The outside of the building represents a balanced synthesis of Renaissance and Baroque styles which make it one of the most beautiful buildings in the city. The two longer sides, towards piazza San Fedele and La Scala, have three floors; the shorter ones two. The bottom

Here, the statue of Leonardo da Vinci with Palazzo Marino, covered for the 1989 restorations, in the background. Above and on the next page, the inner courtyard of Palazzo Marino, with its double-column portico.

floor is in the Doric style, with windows flanked by a (spalle bagnate) column; the second floor has window with broken-curve tympanums interposed with fluted pilaster strips; the last floor has windows with triangular tympanums. Each side is broken up by elegant portals.

Inside, the court of honor is lined with a portico supported by coupled columns. On the upper floor there is a loggia with round arches. Only the Alessi hall may be visited.

CHURCH OF SAN FEDELE

It faces the square of the same name, which in the last century was expanded to include the area thata once held Palazzo Stannazzari, the home of Giuseppe Prina destroyed during the tumults which broke out after his death. The parvis of the church has held a work by Barzaghi since 1883, the monument to an old an tired Alessandro Manzoni who died after a fall from the steps of this very temple.

This church, one of the most beautiful examples of cinquecento architecture, was built in 1569 under instruction by Carlo Borromeo based on a design by Pellegrini; the façade was completed a couple of decades later by Martino Bassi, while Richini built the crypt and choir loft in the first half of the 1600's. Home to the Jesuits, it was supported for a certain period by the Canons of Santa Maria della Scala, who had seen their church demolished to make way for the building of the La Scala Theatre; it then became a ducal chapel for a few years, known as the church of Santa Maria della Scala at San Fedele.

At the center of the monumental façade, topped by a triangular pediment, a Baroque portal with an arched tympanum and the second-floor window are inserted, flanked by statues and friezes interposed with columns. The left side, with two rows of columns interposed with niches and statues, fascinated Stendhal.

Inside there is a single nave with majestic red granite columns. The chapel arches are flanked by two rows of smaller arches: the upper row acts as a women's gallery, the lower holds eight beautifully crafted wooden confessionals made between 1596 and 1603 by Giacomo, Giovanni and Giampaolo Taurini. The sacristy is also lovely, with the carved-wooden cabinets by Daniele Ferrari, a Jesuit student of Giovanni Taurini. The main altar, pavilion-style, is the work of Pietro Pestagalli. Next to the presbytery, a corridor leads to the chapel of Madonna dei Torriani, with an ancient Marian painting once found in the nearby demolished church of San Giovanni delle

Above, the frieze on the large triangular pediment of the church of San fedele, and an anthropomorphous sculpture under the curved tympanum.
On the facing page, the monument to Alessandro Manzoni (1883), with the façade of San Fedele in the background.

Case Rotte. The "case rotte" or "broken houses" refer to those of the Torriani family, destroyed after the advent of the Viscontis.

MANZONI HOUSE

At nr. 1 of via Morone we find the house of Alessandro Manzoni, who lived there from 1814 to his death in May 1873. The Risorgimento-style building houses the National Center of Manzoni Studies.

On the ground floor are the rooms of the poet's house which are still intact. On the upper floor there is the bedroom with its original furniture and a small museum with historical documents and personal items. The ground floor also holds the Lombard Historical Society, with the Lombard historical archives and a specialized library.

Piazza Belgioioso, in front of the Manzoni House, is bordered by the splendid Palazzo Belgioioso and connects to piazza Meda through an archway: in the flower bed, Arnaldo Pomodoro's rotating sundial.

Hours: Tuesday, Wednesday, Thursday, Friday 9 a.m. - 12 noon/2-4 p.m. *Closed holidays.*

POLDI PEZZOLI MUSEUM

The Poldi Pezzoli Museum, 12 via Manzoni, was created by the Milanese gentleman Gian Giacomo Poldi Pezzoli, who arranged his own collections in the vast rooms of his home. Upon his death, this valuable and unique collection of art, one of the most important in the world, was donated to the city of Milan according to the wishes of its founder, who had instituted an independent artistic foundation, willing the house and the collections for public benefit so that the order and organization he began would be maintained.

The collection, which Gian Giacomo Poldi Pezzoli and originally conceived only for arms, thanks to the influence of his mother, the Marchesa Rosina Trivulzio, was expanded to include many other subjects such as gold, jewels, glass, fabrics, furniture, sculpture, also following the advice of artists such as Molteni and Bertini and art historians such as Giovanni Morelli.

The museum was closed during the war of 1915-1918, and its re-opening was financed by public organizations and by the Milanese upper class, who still support the museum today. Damaged during the second world war, it returned to operation in 1951. The museum occupies over twenty rooms on the two floors of Palazzo Porta.

GROUND FLOOR. The antique Arms room, which holds arms of every kind and from every period.

ROOM III. Also called the Fresco due to the painting depicting the *Glorification of Bartolomeo Colleoni* by Carlo Carlone which decorates the ceiling; here are gathered fabrics, holy vestments, brocades, and two altar-facings from the late 15th century, originally from Santa Maria delle Grazie with drawings probably of the Da Vinci school.

ROOM IV or ARCHEOLOGY ROOM. Here we find objects of all kinds, including a lovely Tabriz rug of the XVI century with mythological figures.

ROOM V. Holds the library.

ROOM VI. Consists of the vestibule, with a II-century Roman sarcophagus, and the stairs leading to the *piano nobile*, where the sequence of rooms continues.

ROOM VII. Consists of the second floor vestibule and contains two busts by Canova and Lorenzo Bartolini.

Behind the Manzoni House at nr. 3 via Degli Omenoni we find the house known as "Omenoni", which takes its name from the eight giants sculpted into its façade, two of which support the second-floor architrave and are known by the Milanese as "omenoni", or "big men".

They were sculpted by Antonio Abbondio in the second half of the 16th century following a drawing buy the sculptor Leone Leoni, who lived and worked in that house, which we designed. The eight telamones on the upper floor are topped by the same number of Ionic columns, half-embedded in the wall and interposed with windows. The top floor was built in the last century. Under the cornice, a sculpture symbolizing *Slander torn to pieces by lions.*

On the facing page, two details of the Omenoni House, huge XVI-century sculptures. Above, the entrance to the Manzoni House.

*Above, an interior of the Poldi-Pezzoli Museum; left, the
Tabriz tapestry from the XVI century with mythological il-
lustrations.
On the facing page, St. Francis and the Christ by Crivelli.*

50

On the facing page, Madonna with child by Andrea Mantegna.
Above left, Madonna with child by Giovanni Boltraffio; right, the Pietà by Sandro Botticelli. On the following pages: Portrait of a young woman by Antonio Pollaiolo and Madonna with child by Sandro Botticelli.

ROOM VIII or LOMBARD ROOM. Here we find paintings of the XV and XVI-century Lombard school. The most important are: *Madonna with Child* by Vincenzo Foppa, *Madonna with Child and the Lamb* by Cesare da Sesto, *Rest during the flight to Egypt* by Andrea Solari, *Madonna with Child picking a flower by Antonio Boltraffio, Mystical Nuptials of St. Catherine of Alexandria* by Bernardino Luini, in addition to many minor works by these and other artists.

ROOM IX or FOREIGNERS' ROOM. Here are kept works by German and Flemish artists from the XV to the XVIII century, including a beautiful 16th-century tapestry depicting the *Meeting of Esther and Ahasuerus*, hand-made in Brussels, and paintings by Mathys van Hellemont, Nicolaus Alexander Mair, Lucas Cranach the Elder and others.

ROOM X. Left intact with its original decoration, among other items it contains an equestrian statue of Augustus.

ROOM XI or GOLD ROOM. Originally a sales room, it numbers among its most famous

pieces: a Persian rug with hunting scenes and the
valuable tea services and porcelain objects, the
paintings *Gray Lagoon* by Francesco Guardi,
Portrait of a Woman by Antonio del Pollaiolo,
St. Nicholas of Tolentino by Piero della Francesca, *Madonna with Child* and *Mourning for*

Death of St. Jerome by Giovanni Battista Tiepolo.

Christ's Death by Sandro Botticelli, *Imago pietatis* by Giovanni Bellini and *Madonna with Child* by Andrea Mantegna, all masterpieces of Italian painting.

ROOM XII. Hosts works from the collections of Emilio Visconti Venosta, such as the *Madonna with Child* by Bergognone and *Madonna with Child* and San Giovannino by Pinturicchio.

ROOM XIII or WATCH ROOM. Here the valuable collection donated by Bruno Falck is displayed, including one hundred twenty-nine watches, including some solar watches and one armillary sphere.

ROOM XV or BLACK ROOM. Includes extremely valuable furnishings and paintings of significant importance.

ROOM XVI or ANTIQUE MURANO GLASS ROOM. This was Gian Giacomo Poldi Pezzoli's bedroom and, in addition to the precious glass works, it also holds paintings and valuable furnishings.

ROOM XVII. The Dante Room, which has remained intact, decorated with windows and frescoes.

ROOM XVIII. Among other works, it holds the *Portrait of a Courtesan* by Jacopo Palma the Elder.

ROOM XIX and XX. Here are displayed 16th and 17th-century paintings, a collection of bronzes and two tapestries.

ROOM XXI or GOLD LAVATORY. Was once the washroom, and today holds gold and various kinds of valuable items.

ROOM XXII. Holds 18th-century Venetian painters, including Guardi and Canaletto.

ROOM XXIII. Here works by Perugino are displayed.

The visit ends with ROOM XXIV or the VENETIAN ROOM, in which works by masters of the XV and XVI century, including Bellini and Lotto, are displayed.

Hours: Tuesday, Wednesday, Thursday, Friday and Sunday: 8:30 a.m. - 12:30 p.m. /2:30-6:00 p.m.; *Saturday*: 9:30 a.m.-12:30 p.m. / 2:30-7:30 p.m. *Closed Mondays.*

PALAZZO CLERICI

At number 5 via Clerici we find one of the most beautiful and sumptuos patrician homes of Milan, from which the street takes its name. The elegant residence was built, using an old pre-existing structure, per the wishes of the marshall Antonio Giorgio Clerici in the early 1700's. From 1773 to 1778 the building was adapted to hold the Court, and in 1813 it was sold to the State, who chose it as the seat for the Court of Appeals until 1940. It currently houses the Institute for the Study of World Politics, whom it is necessary to ask for permission to visit the interior.

The construction consists of two long side wings, interrupted by elegant windows and by a central body, well-retracted to allow carriages to pass from the main gate, inserted in a portal with a curved tympanum and decorated by a stucco seashell.

The inner courtyard has a porticoed area, supported by coupled Tuscan columns, and is decorated by wrought-iron window sills. To the right stands the famous honor staircase with three ramps, whose unique feature consists of the corner pilasters in the form of Oriental female figures.

On this and the following pages, an overall view and details of the frescoes by Giovanni Battista Tiepolo in Palazzo Clerici, protraying the Carriage of the Sun.

The stair is topped by a frescoed medallion on the vault, attributed to G.B. Piazzetta.

The most interesting part of the building is the Tapestry Gallery. On the walls, sparkling with mirrors, one can admire four XVII-century Flemish tapestries: *Moses in the presence of the Pharaoh, Crossing the Red Sea, Battle of the Amalekits and Moses and Jethro's daughter.* The ceiling is covered with magnificent frescoes by Tiepolo from 1740 the *Carriage of the Sun* which, guided by Mercury, illuminates the world; at his sides Venus, Saturn, Mars, Ceres, Favonius, gods of the heavens and seas surrounded by dolphins, water-nymphs and tritons, and the continents with human and animal figures.

CIVIC MUSEUM OF CONTEMPORARY HISTORY

Located on the ground floor of the Palazzo Morando Attendolo Bolognini, 6 via Sant'Andrea, the museum was inaugurated in 1963 and gathers documents and historical curios from the beginning of the first world war to the end of the second. The interior and displays were designed by the architects Matilde Baffa, Luca Meda, Ugo Rivolta and Aldo Rossi. A painting by Aldo Carpi is found at the entrance to the museum.

ROOM I. Here we find testimonies to the first phase of the Great War, during the period when Italy was neutral, and of the first interventions, including a coded telegram dated May 24, 1915 sent by General Cadorna to the Allies to inform them of the Italian intervention, and Vittorio Emanuele II's signed proclamation to the troops, again dated May 24, the first day of the war.

ROOM II. Gathers documents from 1916-17, including the telegram from Cadorna to General Joffre which heralds the Austrian offensive in Trentino, the bronze by Luigi Secchi *The messenger girl*, and a painting by Augusto Colombo about the *Martyrdom of Cesare Battisti.*

ROOM III. Here we find a model of the trenches, banners, arms and fragments of bombs launched on Milan by the Austrians.

ROOM IV. The battle of the Piave and the battle of Vittorio Veneto are documented, as well as the armistice of November 4, 1918. The Austrian battleship "Viribus Unitis", sunk by the italian MAS, is also remembered.

ROOM V. Gathers documents and memorabilia, also from the post-war period, including some about the birth of Fascism.

ROOM VI. Gathers documents about the Fascists' rise to power and the conquest of Ethiopia.

ROOM VII. Documents the Spanish Civil War and the assassination of the brothers Aldo an Carlo Rosselli.

ROOMS VIII and IX. Here are kept documents on the Second World War up to the referendum of June 1948.

ROOM X. Collection of arms and uniforms from the Second World War.

Hours: 9:30 a.m. - 12:30 p.m. / 2:30-5:15 p.m. *Closed Mondays.*

MUSEUM OF MILAN

On the second floor of the Palazzo Morando Attendolo Bolognini in via Sant'Andrea, which houses the Museum of Contemporary History. It is arranged in a large apartment, where one can admire furniture and household items from 18th-century Milan. Documents and paintings which narrate the events of the city from its origins to our time are preserved here. It was instituted in 1935.

It covers twenty rooms, not all of which are open to the public; the last occasionally hosts exhibits and shows.

Among the most important paintings in the collection: *The laying of the first stone of the Vittorio Emanuele Galleria* by Domenico Induno, paintings by Bossoli, Durini, De Albertis, Migliara, Campi, the famous *Servants' Passage* by Giuseppe Canelli, paintings dedicated to the Five Days of Milan, the *Piazza del Duomo* by Angelo Inganni.

There are many busts and portraits of famous people such as Beccaria, Parini, Porta, signboards of shops and shows, notices of the first trams and trains, maps and prints of old Milan complete the collection.

Hours: 9:30 a.m. - 12.20 p.m. / 2:30-5:15 p.m. *Closed Mondays.*

On the facing page, a frescoed room in the Civic Museum of Contemporary History. Above, the courtyard of Palazzo Morando Attendolo Bolognini, which houses the Museum of Contemporary History and the Museum of Milan.

ITINERARY Nr. 2: THE AMBROSIAN AREA

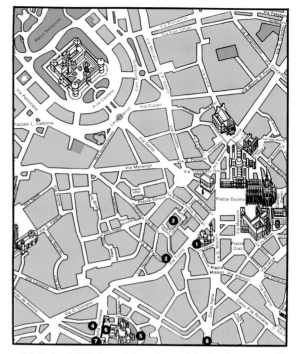

CHURCH OF SANTA MARIA AT SAN SATIRO

Located between via Torino and via Falcone. The original nucleus dates back to approximately 876 when the archbishop of Milan, Ansperto da Biassono, had a church built in honor of San Satiro, the brother of St. Ambrose. In 1478 it was assigned to Donato Bramante. Bramante saved and incorporated only one apse, known as the sacellum of San Satiro or Chapel of Mercy, and the romanesque-Lombard bell tower.

The main façade facing via Torino was probably begun by Giovanni Antonio Amadeo, but remained incomplete due to conflicts with Bramante. It was not completed until the second half of the 1800's in a pseudo-Baroque style. The rear façade, which opens onto via Falcone, is the 15th-century work of Bramantino, and the cylindrical exterior of the sacellum of San Satiro stands out, carved with niches and topped by the 15th-century lantern. This side is broken by two Doric portals from 1517, crowned by a tympanum, the work of Giovan Antonio of Oggiono.

Next to the sacellum is the beautiful bell tower built at the end of the X century, perhaps the city's oldest, which holds Roman remains in its base. Hanging cornices and arches divide it into four floors, decorated with architectural motifs.

The false perspective of the apse, designed to compensate the lack of space and give the illusion of depth, is the fruit of Bramante's genius. The presbytery, which is actually about one meter deep, from the church entrance appears to be a true apse.

In the copula one can admire, among other works, a votive fresco of *Madonna with Child,*

Façade of the church of Santa Maria at San Satiro.

which in 1242 is said to have bled when struck by a knife. In the lunette, *Story of the Miracle by Pomerio.* At the end of the right arm there is the ancient Chapel of Mercy cited above, in the form of a four columns. The oldest capitals are from the Carolingian period. Traces of Byzantine frescoes adorn the walls. The chapel takes its name from a colored terracotta group, *La Pietà* (The Mercy), the 15th-century work of Agostino de' Fondutis, located above the altar.

Also precious is the Bramantesque baptistry, exsacristy, entered from a chapel of the right nave. It is octagonal in shape and has rectangular and semicircular niches at its base, interposed with open-book pilaster strips which also continue in the upper part between the decorated biforis windows.

CHURCH OF SAN SEBASTIANO

Continuing along via Torino one comes to the civic church of San Sebastiano, where the city's religious holidays are celebrated. It was built following a votive offering for the end of the plague in 1576 on the site once covered by the chapel of San Quintino. The initial design by Pellegrino Tibaldi was later modified by Martino Bassi, Fabio Mangone and Giuseppe Meda; the latter is responsible for the presbytery, to which the small cupola was added in the 1700's.

The church, round in form, has three portals, one of which is the work of Giacomo Manzù.

The tambour over the interior has eight windows, with modern panes by Piero Marussig. The herms continue in flat ribs into the eight-segmented cupola, with the frescoes by Agostini Pomerio *Evangelists, doctors of the church,* completed by Pasini.

There are four side chapels and one presbytery. The first chapel to the right, known as the "goldsmiths' chapel", preserves on its altar and sides paintings depicting Sant'Eligio, protector of goldsmiths, who bring their works in offering on June 25th. In the second, two works by Montalto depicting *The Annunciation* at the altar and *The slaughter of the innocents* in the lunette. The presbytery covered by a cupola is located in a square room beyond the arcade. Behind the main altar, a walnut root choir loft designed by Carlo Giuseppe Merlo in 1759, above which we find canvasses by Antonio Maria Ruggeri, Federico Bianchi and Andrea Lanzani. To the left of the presbytery arcade is the model for the large statue of St. Francis in piazza Risorgimento, by Trentacoste.

Returning towards the exit, in the second chapel to the left there is a marble work depicting the *Pietà* by Benedetto Cacciatori, and a fresco by Filippo Abbiati in the lunette. The first chapel on the left is completely dedicated to the church's saint. At the altar, a recent copy of a painting by Vincenzo Foppa depicting *St. Sebastian,* to the sides two works by Filippo Abbiati: right, *St. Irene removing arrows from St. Sebastian* and left, *Martyrdom of St. Sebastian.*

AMBROSIAN ART GALLERY

In piazza Pio XI stands the Palazzo dell'Ambrosiana, dating from the XVII century, the site of the library and art gallery, both ordered by the cardinal Federico Borromeo. The Ambrosian Art Gallery gathers especially prestigious paintings, from the original collection donated by Borromeo to those ordered by Gian Alberto Dall'Acqua and Lamberto Vitali in 1966.

Along the staircase leading to the first thirteen rooms — the last is on the ground floor — we find the plaster casts of Michelangelo's *Pietà,* today in the Vatican Basilica, and of the *Laocoonte Rodio,* in the Vatican Museum.

ROOM I. The most important works are the *Madonna of the Canopy* by Botticelli, the *Nativity* by Ghirlandaio, a polyptych from 1486 by Bartolomeo Vivarini, a large pala from 1480 by Bergognone, representing a *Madonna with Child, angels, eight saints and an offerer.*

ROOM II. Gathers some pre-Romanesque sculptures (X and XI c.) from the Benedictine monastery in Cairate (VA), and two *Madonnas with Child,* one by Pseudo Boccaccio, mid-XVI century, and one by Bernardino de' Conti.

ROOM III. Here are kept fragments of the tomb of Gastone di Foix, a sculpture by Bambaia, and frescoes by a Lombard master of the early XVI century depicting saints and bishops.

ROOMS IV, V and VI. These gather works by Flemish and German painters. Included are paintings by Jan Brueghel the Elder (1563-1625): two canvasses of the *Madonna with Garland* and three *Still Lifes,* the two miniatures of the *Fire and water allegory* and twelve pieces of *Paesini.* Of great interest is the triptych by Joos van Cleve depicting the *Adoration of the Magi, Virile portraits* by Hans Mülich, *Fowl* by Jan van Kessel. Also to note are the display cases of curios, including astrolabes, armillary spheres, watches, ivories, bronzes, gold, and a lock of Lucrecia Borgia's hair and her letters from a correspondence with Cardinal Bembo.

ROOM VII. Holds mostly paintings by Lombard painters such as Solario, Giorgione and Bernardino Luini. By Luini, *Young St. John with the Lamb,* the *Madonna of the milk* and drawings. By Bramantino, the first work from 1490 representing the *Adoration of the Child* and a *Pietà,* from a lunette of the church of San Sepulcro.

ROOM VIII. Among the many important works we should mention the *Holy Family* by Luini, the *Madonna of St. Michael* by Bramantino, two *Manger Scenes* by Martino Piazza and Giampietrino. The room is embellished with three famous works of the Da Vinci school: *St. John the Baptist, The Musician,* and *Profile of a Gentlewoman,* perhaps Beatrice d'Este, by Ambrogio de Predis. Here we also find a triptych by Marco d'Oggiorno, *Madonna with Child and the Saint Johns.*

ROOM IX. Contains, among others: Judith by Andrea Fabrizi, Madonna with Child and the Saint Johns by Bugiardini, The washing of the feet by Dossi, one Christ in the Garden by Lomazzo and another by Campi, Holy Family by Sodoma.

On the facing page, above and below, the interior of the Bramantescque sacellum of San Satiro. Far right, above and below, details of the exterior façade of the Ambrosiana.

ROOM X. Holds miniatures and bronzes from the Sinigallia collection, cartoons by Giulio Romano for the *Battle of Constantine* and by Pellegrino Tibaldi for the windows of the Duomo. The rear wall is completely occupied by the famous *Cartoon for the School of Athens* of 1510, the only one remaining of those done by Raphael for the Vatican Rooms. It represents the greatest philosophers and mathematicians in conference, and among the faces some of Raphael's contemporariers are recognizable: Federico II Gonzaga, Francesco della Rovere, Pietro Bembo, Bramante, Sodoma and perhaps Michelangelo. On the door, a copy of Leonardo da Vinci's *Last Supper* by Vespino.

ROOM XI. Gathers famous Baroque paintings, including work by Guido Reni, Spranger, Procaccini, Nuvolone. Very interesting are the two works by Giovan Battista Tiepolo, *Bishop* and *Presentation at the temple*, as well as Caravaggio's celebrated work, *Basket of fruit*. Here we also find the *Adoration of the Magi* by Morazzone and the *Nativity* by Barocci.

ROOM XII. Holds neoclassical works of art: the gold-plated bronze model of the Triumphal Arch by Luigi Cagnoa an the self-depicting marble busts of Canova and Thorwaldsen, paintings by Cigola, Schiavoni, Bossi, Landi, Traballesi, portraits of *Napoleon* and of the *Signora Rua* by Appiani.

ROOM XIII. Here we find some very important works: *Portrait of a knight* from 1554 by Moroni, *Ecce Homo, Adoration of the Magi, Magdalene* and *Portrait of an old warrior* by Titian, *Announcement to the shephards* and *Rest during the flight to Egypt* by Jacopo Bassano and *St. Peter Martyr* by Moretto da Brescia.

The collection ends with the exposition in Room XIV on the ground floor, which holds paintings from 17th-century Lombard Mannerism.

Hours: 9:30 a.m. - 5:00 p.m. *Closed Saturdays.*

The AMBROSIAN LIBRARY, in the same building, is of extreme interest. Among the most valuable documents, the Leonardesque *Atlantic Code*, the *Divine Comedy* from 1353, Arabic manuscripts and Syrian versions of the Bible, 2,500 incunabula. It was the first library in Europe opened to the public.

COLUMNS OF SAN LORENZO

They stand at the end of corso di Porta Ticinese, just before the ancient Porta Ticinese which, together with Porta Nuova at the end of via Manzoni, is the only survivor of the medieval wall, which at one time counted six gates.

They are sixteen Corinthian columns, eight and a half meters high, originally from the II and III century, which perhaps decorated a pagan temple to the goddess Cybele, near piazza Santa Maria Beltrade, and moved here in the IV century when construction began on the basilica of San Lorenzo. They are crowned by a marble architrave interrupted mid-way by a brick arch. At one end is a stone to Lucio Vero from 197 A.D., found in the area in 1600.

BASILICA OF SAN LORENZO

This pre-Christian basilica stands in front of the sixteen Corinthian columns. It was erected spanning the IV and V centuries using marble from ancient Roman buildings, the circus and amphitheatre, which stood nearby, and underwent a number of restructurings and transformations over the centuries. It was in fact rebuilt several times following two fires, in 1071 and 1124, and two collapses, one in 1103 and one in 1572 which involved the cupola. The façade was tampered with again in 1894. In spite of it all, it remains one of the most meaningful and fascinating pre-Christian monuments in Milan and the symbol, also due to the majestic columns in front of it, of Milan's Roman heritage.

Its origins are uncertain: some believe that the original nucleus was an Aryan church, others a Palatine basilica, similar in structure to the mausoleum of San Vitale in Ravenna and the Acquisgrana cathedral ordered built by Charlemagne. Augustine transformed it into a Christian basilica. The ancient quatrefoiled form with its open exedras has been maintained, while frail traces of what must have been splendid mosaics remain.

On the facing page, Basket of fruit by Caravaggio, preserved in the Ambrosiana.
This page, the basilica of San Lorenzo and details of the columns.

The basilica is entered by a three-arched pronaos, a nineteenth-century work by the architect Nava, in which traces of the ancient portals are inserted. The two presbyteries desired by Federico Borromeo extend towards the parvis, at the center of which stands the statue of Constantine.

The central body, consisting of an ample octagonal room, is covered by the octagonal cupola in eight sections, the largest in Milan, rebuilt by Martino Bassi under Carlo Borromeo after the collapse in 1573. The main altar, in the exedra in front of the entrance, is the Baroque work of Carlo Garavaglia, built with ancient marble. Following the ambulatory to the right one comes to a small chapel, a baptistry in Federico Borromeo's time, at whose altar is a panel by Aurelio Luini, *Baptism of Jesus.* Further on and through an atrium, or the Chapel of Our Lady of Sorrows, wich contains precious mosaics, one enters the ancient chapel of Sant'Aquilino, closed by Roman portals from the I century, where the saint's remains are preserved in a silver urn. The octagonal chapel with rectangular and circular niches dates from the IV century, and is one of the most complete and lovely examples of a Romanesque octagonal building. It was probably originally a mausoleum ordered by Galla Placidia, daughter of the emperor Theodoric, who according to tradition was buried in the sarcophagus now in the right niche. The mosaics in the rear niches are quite ancient, perhaps pre-dating those in Ravenna, and depict Christ among the Apostles and the abduction of Elijah, the drawing of which can be glimpsed at the bottom.

From the chapel one descends into the vaults, where the foundations of the basilica, originally from a late-Imperial Roman building, can be seen.

Returning to the ambulatory and continuing the rounds, one encounters the eighteenth-century sacristy and baptistry, and the chapel of the Holy Family under the tower, the internal pilaster of which is decorated by lovely frescoes: *St. Helen,* XII century, and *Madonna with Child,* XIV century.

One then comes to the Cittadini chapel, named for the family which expanded the pre-existing apsidal sacellum, decorated with the remains of frescoes. Behind the main altar, the chapel of Sant'Ippolito, which has unfortunately lost all of its decorations, while retaining its ancient brickwork structure. The exterior is octagonal, semispherical, and supported by four Roman columns with shafts of African marble and Corinthian capitals. This chapel also gives access to the basement vaults, where one may admire the foundations.

Returning to the surface, one proceeds until the next tower, under which we find the 1568 sepulchre of Giovanni del Conte, and then to the last chapel, of San Sisto. Built in the VI century by order of the bishop Lorenzo I, it has the same structure as that of Sant'Aquilino but has lost all decoration. Traces of the ancient pavement and portal can be found in the small atrium before it.

Re-entering the central body, on the right is a fresco of the *Last Supper,* a copy of the one by Leonardo da Vinci which only slightly pre-dates it, and a relief of the church's patron St. Lawrence. In order to view the entire complex of the basilica from the outside, with the chapels and towers, one moves to the rear in piazza Vetra, which offers an enchanting view.

PIAZZA VETRA

The piazza's name perhaps derives from "vetera" or "castra vetera" in remembrance of the ancient Roman encampments or remains found in this area. In this square, before the construction of the Maximilian walls in the fourteenth century, the Nirone and Seveso rivers met to become a single stream of water called the Vettabia. These rivers were deviated after the walls were built in order to be used as a drainage ditch.

In 1955 the remains of a XIV-century bridge were discovered, and in 1960 the abutments of a Roman bridge from the III century. The piazza was the site of capital executions from 1045 to 1840, and long held the reputation of a sinister place.

The basilical park, from which San Lorenzo and the church of Sant'Eustorgio can both be admired, opens to the north.

On the facing page, top, piazza Vetra with the Roman remains; bottom, Porta Ticinese, one of the gates of Milan's medieval walls.

CHURCH OF SANT'EUSTORGIO

Before arriving at Porta Ticinese one comes to the piazzetta di Sant'Eustorgio, come of the most important in Milan. Its origins are controversial: some claim it was built on the spot where Milan's only Christian cemetery and stood for two centuries, under the bishop Eustorgio — whence its name — in the first half of the IV century, as he had selected it as a sanctuary for the relics of the Magi, pulled by an ox-cart from Constantinople. Another version says that the primitive nucleus of the church is what Ambrose called the basilica Portiana. These origins may be confirmed by some pre-Christian remains found beneath the basilica, but other sources say it dates to 515 and was built by the bishop Eustorgio; however, the first reliable documents date back to the VII century. It was destroyed by Barbarossa, who plundered it of the mythical relics of the Magi, and rebuilt in 1190 in Romanesque style. It underwent various transformations over the centuries, especially Baroque additions and nineteenth-century renovations, which were definitively dismantled by 1966, returning to its original Lombard Romanesque style.

The neo-Romanesque façade is from 1865, but still shows the two-storey balcony from 1597, which also held Cardinal Borromeo, built to recall the wooden pulpit from which St. Peter Martyr thundered. The latter was a Dominican inquisitor who had heretics, witches and all sorts of dissidents burned at the stake and tortured and who, stabbed by Catharists, is said to have rested in the splendid Portinari chapel, the Renaissance jewel of the basilica and of the entire city.

The XIII-century bell tower is the tallest in the city.

The three-span interior is divided by cruciform and cylindrical pilasters, slightly inclined outwards giving the impression of a wider central span. The capital of the third pilaster on the right depicts the *Transport of the ark of the magi*.

The first three chapels on the right protrude irregularly. The first, by Angelo Palazzi of Lugano, is from 1484, and has an octagonal lantern and a pitched roof with lamp. It belongs to the Brivio family, and the altar bears a triptych by Bergognone depicting the *Madonna with Child between St. Jacob and St. Augustine* and, on the left wall, the sepulchral monument of Giovanni Stefano Brivio. The second chapel is another early fifteenth-century Gothic work of

Above, the basilica of Sant'Eustorgio. On the facing page, the church's main entrance portal.

the Torelli family. It is decorated with frascoes from the XVII century, while the altar is from the following century. On the left wall, Pietro Torelli's tomb, a Gothic work by Jacopino da Tradate. The third chapel, of the Caimi family, built in the 1500's and re-modelled in the late 1600's, holds frescoes by Sassi. On the left wall, *St. Ambrose on horseback*, a copy of Figino's painting preserved at the Sforza Castle; below, the sarcophagus of Protaso Caimi.

The next four chapels — the fourth, fifth, sixth, and seventh — are aligned and date from the XIV century. The fourth belongs to the Viscontis and is the most important in the church, next to the Portinari chapel discussed below: its walls are covered with valuable frescoes, free from the 17th-century façade which covered them. Particularly refined is a Lombard fresco from the late 1300's depicting *St. George and the dragon*. The majestic sepulchral monument of Stefano Visconti, with a lovely relief of the sarcophagus showing *Saints introducing Stefano Visconti and his wife Valentina Doria to the Virgin*, is attributed to Bonino da Campione. Still to the left, there is a Tuscan-style *Crucifix* from the early 1300's, to which pregnant women were sent when they came down with a fever. The fifth chapel has on its walls large canvasses by Antonio Lucini and one canvas attributed to Gian Battista Crespi, from the late 16th century, depicting *St. Francis in ecstasy before the Madonna with Child*. In the sixth chapel, still of the Viscontis, to the right, sepulchral monument of Gaspare Visconti, which he himself ordered from a follower of the Campionese masters; left, the sepulchral monument of Umberto III Visconti and, below, the tombstone of Agnese Besozzi, second wife of Gaspare.

The vault of the seventh chapel, of the Torrianis, contains a fresco from the school of Michelino da Besozzo, XV century.

The eighth holds a large late-Romanesque sarcophagus where according to legend the remains of the Magi kings, to which the chapel is dedicated, were preserved, then purloined and taken to the Cologne cathedral in 1164 by the archbishop Reinold von Dassel, and restored in small part in 1903. The relics are now kept in an urn in the chapel. On the altar mensa is a precious marble triptych by Giovanni di Balduccio or a Campionese master. On the right wall of the right transept is the large canvas by Storer depicting *The slaughter of the innocents*, and on the left wall *Ephiphany*, a 15th-century fresco attributed to Luini.

Leaving the Magi chapel one arrives at the prized marble triptych, perhaps donated by Gian Galeazzo Visconti, divided into nine panels depicting the *Story of the passion* and with reliefs of the Apostles. The modern urn beneath the altar contains the remains of Eustorgio, Onorato and Magno, Milanese bishops.

The pseudo-crypt behind the main altar was built in 1537 using the nine columns from the Pilgrim hostel which stood in front of the cloister of the nearby convent. Restorations have brought to light a section of pre-Christian wall. The frescoes on the wall, by Carlo Urbini, are from 1578.

The seven chapels of the left nave contain frescoes which were once in the upper chancel. We should point out the 14th-century *Madonna with Child* of the fifth chapel (counting from the entrance), where we also find the tombstone of the bishop Federico Maggi, who died in 1333.

Returning to the pseudocrypt, one proceeds along a corridor with detached frescoes from the 1300's and a statue of St. Eugene in multi-colored stone. On then arrives in a long vestibule which opens into two 15th-century-Gothic chapels. In the right one, belonging to the Arluno family, presbytery, with the main altar decorated by a

a Giottesque fresco depicting *St. Dominic in prayer, St. Francis* and a *Deposition*. The other chapel, of the Crisolora family, has frescoes by Daniele Crespi in the second bay.

One thus reaches the splendid appendix to the church, the Portinari chapel, and extremely refined and elaborate Renaissance monument. It was erected between 1462 and 1466 under the direction of Pigello Portinari, a procurator for the Medici Bank in Milan, to house the remains of that St. Peter Martyr murdered by the Catharists and thereby ingratiate himself with Bianca Maria, wife of Francesco Sforza, dedicated to the saint.

The artist of the chapel is not known for sure: it could be either the Florentine Michelozzo or Filarete. The layout, with its two square rooms, one larger and one smaller for the altar, recalls the one by Brunello and is elaborated according to the canons for gold sections learned from the Florentine master. The colorful decorations are the work of Lombard masters. The lower part, separate from the upper part, is decorated by a fired-brick cornice with cherub heads, and the tambour is embellished with dancing angels in stucco, perhaps done by Foppa. This artist also created the magnificent frescoes from 1465 which adorn the upper part of the walls, and which in the past had been covered over the centuries by layers of plaster and other Baroque frescoes. An accidental collapse led to their discovery in 1871 and they were finally restored by the master Mauro Pellicciòli in 1952.

In the lunette over the entrance is the *Assumption of Mary*, in fron the *Annunciation*; in the large lunettes are illustrated *Scenes from the life of St. Peter Martyr*; at right, *St. Peter invoking a cloud to shade the faithful from the sun*, and *St. Peter chasing the devil from the statue of the Madonna with Child;* to the left, the *Saint performing the miracle of Narni and Death of the Saint*; in the pendentive of the cupola, *Doctors fo the Church*.

At the center stands the solemn ark of St. Peter martyr holding the remains of the inquisitor, an early 14th-century work by Giovanni da Balduccio. The ark is richly ornamented with bas-reliefs and supported by pilasters and statues. The sarcophagus is crowned by an aedicula with three cuspids holding statues of the Madonna and saints.

In the chapel to the left of the sacellum is the crystal urn with the skull of the saint, which is said to have been separated from the rest of the body by Giovanni Visconti who wanted it for himself. Still according to legend, Visconti was then struck by terrible migraines, which ceased only when he returned the stolen item: thus was urn holdin the skull as a cure for headaches.

Not to be missed, the final stop of a visit to Sant'Eustorgio must include a tour around the underground Roman and pre-Christian cemetery, which holds the burial tombs, some with human remains, cremation urns, ceramics and a small lapidary with pagan and Christian engravings.

CHURCH OF SANTA MARIA DEI MIRACOLI AT SAN CELSO

The church stands in corso Italia in an area once called the Field of the Three Moores, where at the end of the IV century Ambrose found the remains of two martyrs, Nazarus and Celsus. Another basilica was dedicated to St. Nazarus, while the first church erected to protect a miraculous effigy of the Madonna was named after St. Celsus and located where the bodies were found. Thanks to the offerings of the great multitude of worshippers, it was then possible to build the large adjacent basilica of Santa Maria dei Miracoli.

San Celso was erected in 996 by order to the archbishop Landolfo II. Its façade was made more Baroque in 1651, and in 1818 a bay was demolished to make it possible to build Santa Maria. The current façade was rebuild in 1851 and preserves the arched portal from the X century, a contemporary of the lovely Romanesque bell tower, one of the city's oldest and most fascinating.

The interior has lost many of its frescoes and retains a large pre-Christian sarcophagus as its altar. On the south wall towards the garden we find Lombard pilasters, arches, capitals and other testimonies of the ancient church.

Santa Maria dei Miracoli was built in 1493 and underwent the intervention of many architects. Thi first was Gian Giacomo Dolcebuone, together with Giovanni Antonio Amedeio, arist of the beautiful polygonal apse and the octagonal lantern, followed by Cristoforo Solari, Cesare Cesariano, who had designed the porticoed atrium in front of the church and the façade, later built by Vincenzo Sergni and remodelled once again by Alessi and Martino Bassi in the 1500's.

The interior is in a Latin cross layout and has lateral naves leading to the ambulatory around the presbytery, in which the splendid wooden choir stalls by Galeazzo Alessi are found. born the tradition of touching one's head to the

Inside the façade, the rich organ rests on two caryatids sculpted by Antonio Abbondio di Vig-

View of the church of Santa Maria dei Miracoli at San Celso.

giù. The pavement designed by Martino Bassi on a background of Candoglia marble, which repeats the segments of the cupola above, is very refined.

In the niches of the tambour supporting the cupola, statues of the *Apostles*, modelled in plaster by Agostino de Fondutis in 1503. In the niches of the Madonna altar, covered with silver foil, two works by Annibale Fontana, buried here: the statue of *Our Lady of the Assumption* and the solid gold bas-relief of the *Pietà* at the base. Behind the frontal of the Madonna altar in silver foil are the faded remains of the miraculous fresco which gave the church its name. The main altar is inlaid with hard stones and bronze.

In the third chapel to the right are the woden *Crucifix* of the XV century, which is thought to have been carried on St. Charles' shoulders durign the plague, and the urn of St. Celsus under the mensa.

The altar of the right transept preserves a beautiful work by Paris Bordone, *Holy Family and St. Jerome*.

In the ambulatory we find many paintings and sculptures of great value by artists such as Callistro Piazza, Antonio Campi, and Gaudenzio Ferrari.

At the altar of the left transept is a pre-Christian sarcophagus of the V century, where Ambrose may have laid the body of St. Celsus. The left nave is also filled with works of great value, such s the *Martyrdom of St. Catherine of Alexandria* by Cerano in the third chapel (from the entrance), and in the first chapel a pala by Bergognone depicting the *Virgin adoring the Child and saints.*

The sacristes hold precious works and the church's treasure, closed in walnut cabinets.

DOCKYARD AND CANALS

West of piazza XXIV Maggio we find the Dockyard, a mirror of water into which flow the Olona, now covered, and the Naviglio Grande (Grand Canal), source of the Pavian and Ticinello canals.

Measuring approximately 750 meters in length, 20 in width, it is 1.5 meters deep and has an overall surface of 17,500 sq.m.

The dockyard was constructed in 1603 by the Spanish governor the count of Fuentes, and the work done in 1920 gave it its current structure. Popularly known as the "port of Milan", it was much used for transport in past centuries and is still used for unloading sand and gravel and as a port for tourist boats. As we said, the Grand Canal flows into it, a derivative of the Ticino, on which work was begun around 1178 and which gained fundamental economic importance over the centuries. The Grand Canal is the first and most important of the Milanece canals: it was also decisive in the construction of the Duomo, used to transport the Candoglia marble.

It remains, however, an enchanting corner of Milan, out of the way of its frenetic lifestyle: the Vicolo delle Lavandaie is charming, with its antique wash-houses with their wooden roofs, located to the right of the Canal coming from the Dockyard.

Above, another view of Santa Maria dei Miracoli at San Celso. On the facing page, above, the Dockyard; below, vicolo delle Lavandaie.

ITINERARY Nr. 3: FROM THE UNIVERSITY TO BRERA

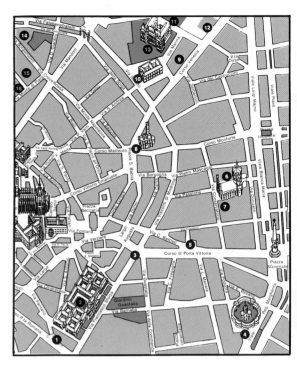

CA' GRANDA, EX MAIN HOSPITAL

Located between via Festa del Perdono and via Francesco Sforza, today it is known as the State University, housed there. It is a grandiose building, easily identifiable in the city, covering an area of 43,00 square meters and 282 meters long.

Originally built as a hospital, it was instituted on April 12, 1456 by Francesco Sforza, and his wife Bianca Maria in order to gather all of the city's small hospitals under a single roof. In relation to the period in which it was built, several important hygienic standards were observed: the sanitary services and storage were located in the basement, far from the patients, the canal behind it collected the discharge from the sewers, and the rooms of the hospital had high ceilings to ensure good ventilation. Men and women were separated, while patients suffering from every kind of disease shared the same areas. It was the site of the hospital until 1939, when it was abandoned for the new Niguarda Hospital. By the time the building was partially destroyed by bombings in 1943, it was uninhabited.

The original design of the hospital was as-signed to a Florentine architect, Antonio Averulino, known as Filarete, recommended to Sforza by Cosimo de' Medici, and he built the first body of the hospital near San Nazaro. He was succeeded by Solari, who raised it with a loggia, while Giovan Antonio Amadeo refinished this first part. The work continued throughout the following century and in 1624, thanks to donations left by Carcano, the hospital was expanded with a courtyard, the work of Richini from drawings by Filarete and Amedeo, entered through a coupled portal crowned by a tympanum, and with the rest of the central building, on which artists such as Fabio Mangone, Giovan Battista Pessina and Corano collaborated. The left wing of the building was built thanks to the donations left by Macchio in 1797, and is sharply differentiated from the rest with its brick-colored plaster work. In 1953 it was faithfully reconstructed by the architects Piero Portaluppi and Liliana Grassi.

Moving to the 17th-century door, one enters into the Richini's courtyard, with its arcaded portico topped by the elegantly decorated gallery. To the right we find the four courtyards by Filarete: the Spicery courtyard, the oldest and least

A view of the former Main Hospital, today the site of the State University.

damaged by the bombs, surrounded by a double row of galleries placed one over the other; the courtyard of the women's baths, also with double galleries, the woodshed courtyard and then the ice-house courtyard. The four courts are bordered by the large cross-vault by Filarete topped by a lantern. Returning to the main courtyard, one finds the 17th-century church of L'Annunciata, and to the left one enters the Macchio wing.

CHURCH OF SAN NAZARO

Located in the square of the same name, approximately half-way down corso di Porta Romana, it was built in 382 by order of Ambrose, who in 196 transferred the bones of the martyr Nazarus there, found together with those of St. Celsus in the Field of the Three Moores. In 1075, following a fire, it was rebuilt in Romanesque style using the pre-Christian perimetral walls; in 1571 it underwent other transformations by order of Carlo Borromeo, who had new windows opened, some chapels removed and the pre-Christian altar moved under the lantern. It was changed and expanded once again in the XVII century, and in the 1800's the interior took on a neoclassical appearance. Finally, the restoration works in 1952 and 1962 dismantled most of the Baroque and neoclassical interventions, uncovering the Romanesque building from the XI century, part of the pre-Christian brickwork, as well as a small ancient bas-relief, perhaps depicting Nazarus himself.

Before entering the church one crosses the Trivulzio chapel, which has its Romanesque façade, built in 1512 by Bramantino under the order of Gian Giacomo Trivulzio, hidden forever. This is Bramantino's only architectural work, although unfinished. Its octagonal interior is crowned by a cupola. Inside we find the arcosoliums, or tombs consisting of arks set into the wall and topped by arches, of those resting here. The statue of Gian Giacomo on the modern entrance bears the famous inscription: "Qui numquam quievit quiescit; tace" (here rests one who never rested; silence). The bones of the Trivulzio family were transported by Carlo Borromeo into the vaults and lost together with hundreds of other corpses in the 1630 plague epidemic.

Descending three steps, which lead to what was ground level in ancient times, one arrives at the church, in Latin cross form, with a single nave and two side arms. In the right transept is the chapel of San Matriano, with traces of the pre-Christian pavement and a canvas by Bernardino Lanino of *The Last Supper*. The lantern is bordered at the corners by the bases of the four pre-Christian pilasters and covered by the cupola. In the apse of the presbytery, the slab on the spot where St. Nazarus was originally buried, whose remains are now kept in an urn under the altar which also contains other relics. In the left transept, a panel by Bernardino Luini showing *Jesus during the Passion* and, at the sides of the porta, a wooden ancon of the school of Adam Kraft of Nuremberg, from the XVI century, depicting the *Manger Scene*. From the left transept one climbs the stairs to reach the 1540 chapel of Santa Caterina, where we find the fresco of the *Martyrdom of St. Catherine*, Linio's masterpiece, in which we can also see the faces of the artist, his teacher Gaudenzio Ferrari and his fellow disciple Giovan Battista della Cerva.

Below, the Sormani Library.
On the facing page, two views of the Besana Rotunda.

PALAZZO SORMANI

The site of the main community Library, it is located in corso di Porta Vittoria at the corner of via Francesco Sforza, and is one of Milan's most important seventeenth-century buildings. The building's outer façade, originally from the 1600's with Baroque work by Francesco Croce from 1736, has a long balustrade and a curved tympanum. The internal façade, built twenty years later, is in the neoclassical style and is the work of Benedetto Alfieri. It has three rows of windows separated by pilaster strips, topped by flat and curved tympanums, and is covered by a balustraded loft, decorated with large classical statues sculpted by Carlo Maria Giudici. The English-style garden was arranged by Leopold Pollack. In the honor hall there are canvasses by Grechetto, depicting Orpheus taming the animals. Since 1956 it has been adapted as a library by the architect Arrigo Arrighetti.

The Periodical Library is also important, with Italian and foreign mastheads, and the Record Library with individual listening stations. Conferences and exhibits of graphic arts, photography and books are often held here.

BESANA ROTUNDA

At'the corner of via Besana and via San Barnaba stands the large monumental complex of San Michele ai Nuovi Sepolcri, also known as Foppone dell'ospedale or the Besana Rotunda. It consists of a circular construction, in brick on the outside and porticoed inside, which surrounds the deconsecrated church of San Michele. The porticoed enclosure was built in 1695 from a design by the engineer Francesco Raffagno, and until 1782 enclosed the cemetery for the deceased from the Main Hospital. In the deep tiled floor of the portico, as many as a hundred and fifty thousand corpses were piled, and only at the beginning of this century was it possible to remove them all and disinfect the area.

Beauharnais' 1809 plan to make it the tample of the Italian Kingdom failed, and the Rotunda was first a lazaretto and later the laundry for the hospital. The church inside, in the shape of a Greek cross, has an altar visible from all of its arms, and is covered by a cupola. The skull decorations of the capitals remind us of the area's original purpose. Now the Rotunda is a public garden, and cultural manifestations are often held there.

CHURCH OF SAN PIETRO IN GESSATE

Located in the square of the same name, in front of the Hall of Justice, it was built thanks to the offerings of the Florentine banker Pigello Portinari between 1447 and 1475, and is the work of Guiniforte Solari and his San Pietro Antonio. It underwent transformations and Baroque additions, and not until 1912 was it restored to its original appearance by Diego Brioschi who, of the many 17th-century re-modellings, left only the baroque sandstone door frame with the sculpture of the church's patron saint in the cymatium.

In the square apse there is the emblem of the benefactors, the Portinari family. The adjacent cloisters were rebuilt in the sixteenth century.

The interior, in a Latin cross shape, has three naves separated by seven pointed arches on each side, resting on granite columns. The church was severely damaged during the war and lost its decorations, of which some traces remain in the left nave.

In the third chapel of the right nave is the *Adoration of the Magi by* Giovan Battista Secchi, in the fifth *The Funerals of St. Martin*, a detached fresco by Borgognone.

In the right transept we find a large wooden Crucifix from the XVII century, and a Leonardesque panel of the *Madonna with Child*.

In the left transept is the Grifi chapel, the most beautiful part of the church. On the vaults and walls is a precious cycle of frescoes showing the *Life of St. Ambrose*, unfortunately badly ruined by the plaster they were covered with in the 1600's. They date back to 1490, as can be deduced by a now-disappeared writing, and are the work of Bernardino Butinone and Bernardino Zenale, from whom they were commissioned by the first notary of the Sforza court, the senator Ambrogio Grifi.

The tomb statue of Ambrogio Grifi, in multicolored marble, stands on the floor of the chapel, and the stone with two medals in relief by Benedetto Briosco adorns the wall.

In the left nave are frescoes attributed to Giovanni Donato Montorfano: in the fifth chapel from the entrance *Stories of the Baptist*, at the altar of the third, the polyptych depicting *Madonna, two saints and offerers, Christ with St. Sebastian and St. Rocco,* and on the walls *Stories of St. Anthony Abbot.*

Above, the church of San Pietro in Gessate and details of the façade.
On the facing page, the church of Santa Maria della Passione.

CHURCH OF SANTA MARIA DELLA PASSIONE

Located at the intersection of via Conservatorio and via Bellini, it is the second-largest church in Milan, after the Duomo. The land on which to build it was donated by the prelate Daniele Birago to the order to the Laterans. The foundations were dug in 1486 and a number of artists were employed in the works that followed: Giovanni Battagio, Cristoforo Lombardi, who in 1530 designed the cupola on a double-row tambour, Martino Bassi who in 1573 designed the naves, transforming the church's layout from a Greek to a Latin cross, and the architect Giuseppe Rusnati, who in 1692 designed the façade. The design of the latter, in a Baroque style adorned with large statues, planned for it to be low enough to allow a view of the lovely cupola. At the base of the pilasters separating the three naves are canvasses by Daniele Crespi and his school, showing half-figures of saints and famous personages from the Order of the Laterans.

The two side naves have six chapels each, all decorated with frescoes, canvasses, and other valuable works. Above the bases of the semi-columns beneath the cupola are paintings by Daniele Crespi reprenting the passion: *Flagellazione, Crowning with Thorns, Ecce Homo, Climb to Calvary, Jesus nailed to the cross, Jesus quenching his thirst, Jesus taken down from the cross and supported by an angel, Angel with the shroud.* The doors of the left organ are also painted by Crespi: inside, *The washing of the feet,* outside *Crucifixion and Descent from the Cross.* Beneath the right organ, the tomb of Daniele and Francesco Birago by Fusiana, from 1495.

In the right transept is a work attributed to Bernardino Luini in 1510, depicting the Descent from the Cross and the Saints Ambrose and Augustine, in the concha of the apse is a fresco by Carlo Urbini from 1550 with *The Marys at the sepulchre and Noli me tangere.* Above the presbytery arch hangs a wooden 15th-century Crucifix, while the main altar is studded with hard stones and multi-colored marble, and has onyx medllions of the pavilioned tabernacle painted by Gilio Cesare Procaccini, Cerano and others. The apse has a carved wooden choir stall with mother-pearl ornaments perhaps designed by Cristoforo Solari, and holds works by Panfilo Nuvolone, the frescoes in the vaults, lunettes and concha, and

large canvasses by Giovanni Francesco Lampugnani. In the left transept are works of great value: at the altar, the *Last Supper*, a panel from 1543 by Gaudenzio Ferrari, enclosed by a frame he may have designed himself, and on the left wall a canvas signed by Giulio Campi and dated 1560, portraying the *Crucifixion*.

Among the many valuable works which decorate the chapels of the left nave, the Fast of St. Charles by Daniele Crespi in the first chapel is of particular interest.

The Basilica Museum also holds significant works.

CONSERVATORY

The rooms of the ex-Lateran Convent, to the right of the church of Santa Maria della Passione, since 1808 have been occupied by the Giuseppe Verdi Conservatory of Music, founded by Eugenio Beauharnais. The arcade of the internal square courtyard has eight arches per side, and the upper floor is separated by Ionic pilaster strips. It was repaired in the post-war period by Reggiori, as it was severely damaged. It includes two halls, a smaller one for chamber music and a larger one for symphonic and choral music, a rich library, and a small museum of valuable stringed instruments.

Above, the façade of the Conservatory.
On the facing page, above, the church of San Babila; below, Palazzo Serbelloni.

CHURCH OF SAN BABILA

Located in the square of the same name and built in the XI century over a pre-existing IV-century basilica called the *ad Concilium Sanctorum*, which perhaps occupied the area of an ancient pagan temple dedicated to the Sun god. The original structure was altered by Renaissance and Baroque remodelings, and especially by the early 20th-century restorations by Cesa Bianchi in a pseudo-Romanesque key. Inside, in the three naves, some medieval capitals are still visible, and the octagonal cupola is decorated with modern mosaics.

In the parvis of the church stands the columns raised by the Serbelloni family in 1600 and holding a Romanesque lion, the symbol of the ancient district of the Eastern gate.

PALAZZO SERBELLONI

At nr. 16 of Corso Venezia stands one of Milan's most important neoclassical buildings. It was ordered in 1793 by the Serbelloni Dukes from the architect Simone Cantoni, who expanded a pre-existing 17th-century palace, of which the side facing via san Damiano remains intact. It hosted a number of illustrious guests: Napoleon with his wife Josephine in 1796, Metternich in

1838, Vittorio Emanuele II and Napoleon III in 1859. Giuseppe Parini taught the sons of the master of the household for some time. At the center of the longer side facing corso Venezia, a large gallery stands out which is supported on two tympanum-topped pillars and divided by pilasters. The irregular shape of the interior has been placed in evidence by replacing the large porch with a series of porticos and rooms leading to the garden. Seriously damaged by bombings in 1943, during which a precious library was also lost, today it is the home of the Press Club, where conferences, debates and manifestations are held.

PALAZZO DEL SENATO

Located in the street of the same name, today it houses the State Archives. It was built over an ex-monastery in 1608 by the architect Fabio Mangone, and later by Francesco Maria Richini. The latter is responsible for the indented façade, built in that manner in order to recover the space lost due to the Canal, now covered, which flowed below. The work was then continued by Gerolamo Quadrio and was not finished until the end of the 1700's. On of the main buildings of the Counter-Reformation, it was ordered by Federico Borromeo, who wished to install the Helvetic College there, dedicated to the training of Swiss clergy in the diocese of Milan. The palace faced the now-covered Canal. In 1787, the Helvetic College was squeezed out by the Josephine reforms and it became the seat of the Government, the Senate, and finally, in 1872, of the State Archives, one of the most complete in Italy with its documents dating as far back as 721, narrating over a millenium of Milanese history.

When it became the seat of the government, the church that stood to the right, the work of Mangone, was dismantled. The corners of the indented façade are covered by rusticated blocks, and the majestic portal is flanked by Ionic columns. To the left of the portal is the first Milanese mailbox, form Napoleon's era. Of significant interest are the two large internal courts, rectangular and co-axial, of the Tuscan order in the lower part and Ionic above.

PUBLIC GARDENS

Covering the area between corso Venezia, Via Palestro, piazza Cavour, via Manin and the bastions of Porta Venezia with their 177,000 square meters, they are one of the few "green lungs" of Milan. Part of their greenery is that of the two convents, of the Carcanines and San Dionigi, which once stood in that area. They were transformed by Giuseppe Piermarini in 1784 according to the canons of the Italian garden, and in such a way that a stair led towards the bastions of Porta Venezia.

In 1857, under Joseph of Austria, Palazzo Dugnani was also incorporated together with its park, which was arranged as an English garden with waterfalls, man-made hills, and ponds by Giuseppe Balzaretto and Emilio Alemagna.

It has always been used as an area for fun and recreation, and enriched with playground rides. After the Unification of Italy it hosted the major merchandise expositions in 1871, '72, and '81. The northwestern portion holds a zoo, now partially dismantled. Within the park are found majestic specimens of exotic plants such as cedars from Lebanon, the Himalayas and the Atlas Mountains.

Here we also find the Monte Merlo hill, and ten monuments to personages of nineteenth-century Milan.

To the south-west is the PLANETARIUM, immediately identifiable due to its large dome, built in 1920 by the architect Portaluppi to contain the sophisticated equipment which simulate the heavens, stars and planets, purchased in Switzerland by the publisher Ulrico Hoepli and do-

Right, the Planetarium.
Facing page, the gardens at Porta Venezia.

nated by him to the City of Milan. It can hold up to 600 people, and interesting conferences and projections regarding the movements of the heavently bodies are held here.

On the western side, towards via Manin, we find PALAZZO DUGNANI, the large patrician residence — one of the few outside the medieval walls — built in the XVII century and re-elaborated in Rococo style in the second half of the following century. Before the French Revolution, sumptuous parties and worldly gatherings were held here. In 1762 it was the seat of the Phoenician Academy, a renowned cultural institution which brought together the intellectuals of the period.

After 1863 it passed to the City of Milan, which first used it as a Museum of Natural History, later moved, and then to host the Alessandro Manzoni Civic High School for Girls. The building consists of a single large body, with the indented side in the center towards the gardens. The inner rooms are elegantly decorated with stuccos and medallions.

Of great interest is the central hall arranged on two floors, containing important frescoes by Gian Battista Tiepolo: *Allegorical Composition of the Dugnani family* and *Stories of Scipione and Massinissa*.

As soon as one enters the Public Gardens from the entrance in corso di Porta Venezia, one faces the huge bulk of the CIVIC MUSEUM OF NATURAL HISTORY.

The building was constructed for this purpose by Giovanni Cerruti on the site of the destroyed Carcanine convent to hold the museum, first housed in Palazzo Dugnani and transferred here in 1893.

The first naturalist collections were granted to the City of Milan by the nobleman Giuseppe de Cristoforis and the professor of botany Giorgio Jan. Among its directors figure prestigious names such as that of the great geologist Antonio Stoppani.

It is in neo-Romanesque style, as dictated by Camillo Boito, and is decorated by iron structures and terracotta. The Museum is also a center of naturalist research. It was destroyed in 1943 in a terrible fire, from which only the collections kept in the vaults were saved, and was re-opened to the public in 1952. On the lower floor are the sections of mineralogy, paleontology, plants, invertebrates and fossils of fish and vertebrates.

A large section is entirely dedicated to dinosaurs, with life-size reconstructions including the American Triceratops. In the Mollusk and Anthropods section there are excellent gigantic specimens, and the entomology section is illustrated with interesting dioramas.

On the second floor we find fish, amphibians, reptiles, birds, and mammals. Some spectacular items: the anaconda, a seven-meter-long snake set in an Amazon background; the skeleton of the rorqual whale beached at Alghero in 1855, nearly twenty meters long and displayed since 1974 suspended in a large hall; the musky ox of the North American arctic tundra; the sperimen of the extinct Quagga, a South Africa zebra of which only about twenty specimens remain in the word's museums; the skeleton of an African elephant, and the background set reconstruction of an enormous male African elephant in motion. The display includes a large collection of bears, tigers, weasels and mammals of all kinds, up to the ape collection.

Facing page, top, Palazzo Dugnani; bottom, a view of pond in the gardens.
Above, the façade of the Museum of Natural History.

Hours: 9:30 a.m. - 12:30 p.m. / 2:30-5:30 p.m. *Closed Mondays.*

VILLA REALE AND THE GALLERY OF MODERN ART

Across via Palestro we find the grandiose Villa Reale, a magnificent example of neoclassical architecture. It was constructed in 1790 on order of the count Lodovico Barbiano di Belgioioso by the architect Leopold Pollack, a favorite student of Piermarini. After the count's death, Napoleon lived there with Josephine, the home donated by the Italian Government, who had taken it over; in 1815 it was passed to Austria, and Radetzky lived there and died there in 1858. Afterwards it belonged to the Savoia family and finally, in 1921, to the City of Milan.

It currently houses the Gallery of Modern Art with the Pavilion of Contemporary Art, the Italian Cinema Museum and the Historical Film Archives. In one room, decorated with magnificent stuccoes, civil marriage ceremonies are held.

The structure of the building, unusual for Milan, recalls Parisian palaces, with the court towards the street and a wall separating it. The side of the villa towards via Palestro is highly sober, while the one facing the garden — the first example of an English garden in the city, animated by stream — is sumptuous and rich in decorations. The interior is the work of Piermarini.

The Gallery of Modern Art, one of the most important in Italy, occupies thirty-five rooms in which nineteenth-century Lombard painting is especially well documented. Among the most representative names, wer can cite Appiani, to whom an entire room is dedicated, Pellizza da Volpedo, with the large canvas of the *Fourth State*, Knoller, Hayez, Carnovali, Faruffini, Cremona, Ranzoni, Mosé Bianchi, Fattori. The sculptures are also by great artists such as Canova, Martini, Marini, Vincenzo Gemito and Medardo Rosso.

The Grassi Collection includes ancient paintings, Oriental works of art and Italian and foreign paintings of the 17th and 18th centuries. We note *The Wait* by Gérard Dou, *Coup de Vent* by Jean Baptiste Corot, *Little girl with flowers* by Michetti, *Great Maneuvers* by Giovanni Fattori, *Clouds at dusk by* Telemaco Signorini, *Washwomen* by Eugéne Bodin, *Interior of lamplight* by Pierre Bonnard, and more works by Segantini, Van Gogh, Cézanne, Toulouse-Lautrec, De Pisis, Boccioni, Gottuso, Casorati.

Hours: 9:30 a.m. - 12:30 p.m. /2:30-5:30 p.m. *Closed Mondays.*

Two photos of the PAC, the Pavillon of Contemporary Art, located in the Gallery of Modern Arts at Villa Reale.

CHURCH OF SAN MARCO

Built in 1254 on the spot where an older chapel had stood, the Milanese dedicated it to St. Mark to thank the Venetians who had helped them to chase out Barbarossa. It was ordered by brother Lanfranco Settala, a general of the order of the Hermits of St. Augustine.

Built in a Romanesque form, it underwent Gothic transformations to the façade, then Baroque interventions on the interior and exterior. This last is still marked by the Baroque style, while the façade is now more Gothic-Lombard in appearance, as conceived by the architect Carlo Maciacchini in 1871. Today all that remains of the old façade is the lovely ogival portal, crowned by an architrave and sculpted by a Campionese master.

The Latin-cross interior layout has three naves; the middle one, 99 meters long, is one of the largest of the Milanese churches. The sepulchral chapels, built after the suppression of the cemetery which was closed to make way for the San Marco pond, open onto the right nave. The sepulchral monuments were largely lost after the enactment of the Council of Trent decree forbidding noblemen from being buried in the churches. Canvasses and frescoes remain in the chapels: in the first, works by Lomazzo from the late 16th century, in the third a pala portraying St. Mark by Legnanino, in the fourth a fresco by Carlo Urbini, in the fifth restored frescoes by Antonio Campi.

Before the right transept is the *Nativity*, a large canvas by Legnanino. Precious frescoes were found in the transept after the Settala tomb was removed in 1956, including the *Crucifixion* by a Lombard master of the late fourteenth century.

The sarcophagus of Settala is also interesting, as are the precious frescoes in the chapel of San Tommaso di Villanova, where we also find the ark of an unknown, attributed to Matteo da Campione or Giovanni da Balduccio. Still in the right transept are the arks of Giacomo Bossi and Martino Aliprandi, by masters of the late 1300's. Near the church's secondary exit (an ex chapel), beneath one fresco was discovered another by a Lombard master, dating back to the second half of the fourteenth century, and portraying *Madonna with St. Augustine and The Aliprandi Family*.

In the presbythery are large canvasses by Procaccini, *St. Ambrose's dispute with St. Augustine* by Cerano, other canvasses by Benovesino from 1617, and the wooden choir area, with sixty-five carved stalls, the work of an Augustinian monk in the XVI century. In the left transept, the chapel of the Pietà is decorated with stuccoes, gold, and frescoes by Montalto.

In the sacristy there are carved cabinets, the *Holy Family and St. Siro* by Bernardino Campi, and canvasses attributed to Legnanino and Montalto.

The left nave, containing the Confessionals, holds works by Campi, Procaccini, and the Lombard Leonardesque shool.

RISORGIMENTO MUSEUM

Located inside Palazzo Moriggia, in via Borgonuovo, it gathers together Italian historical documents, curios, canvasses and sculptures form the end of the 18th century until 1870. Among other items, the first Italian flag delivered by Napoleon to the Lombard League of Mounted Huntsmen, who fought in the French army is kept here; a flag of the Italian Kingdom in gold-threaded silk; the mantle, sceptre and crown taken on by Napoleon on May 26, 1805; the first edition of *My Prisons* by Pellico, Giuseppe Mazzini's writing desk, a collection of Masonic items, the death sentence of Ciro Menotti, the cavalry banner donated by Carlo Alberto to the Milanese women.

Hours: 9:30 a.m. - 12:15 p.m. /2:30-5:30 p.m. *Closed Mondays.*

Facing page, façade of the church of San Marco. Here, a hall in the Risorgimento Museum.

PALAZZO CUSANI

This building stands at nr. 15 of via Brera, and was ordered built by the Marquis Cusani in the XVII century. It later was re-done in Baroque style by Giovanni Ruggeri, who revised the outer façade, while the inner façade, towards the garden, is by Piermarini. After hosting intellectual parties and circles, it was sold by the owners — broke after too much spending — to the Property Office of the Kingdom of Italy, who located the War Ministry there. Today the Commando of the Armed Services are housed here.

The Rococo façade is divided by large Corinthian pilaster strips. On the ground floor there are elegant openworded windows topped by a curved tympanum, in the center of which is an oculum. Two identical sumptuous portals open into the façade, flanked by double pilaster strips, above which stands a stone and wrought-iron balcony.

This sumptuous façade is contrasted by the more severe one which opens onto the garden, built by Piermarini in neoclassical style.

Inside is the courtyard, which maintains its 17th-century appearance and is lined with porticos.

Above, Palazzo Cusani.
Facing page, the courtyard of the Brera Art Gallery.

BRERA ART GALLERY

At via Brera nr. 28, in the same Baroque building, erected between the XV and XVI centuries, that once housed a Humiliati convent, it stands in an uncultivated area known as the "meadow" or "brera".

Today it houses the Fine Arts Academy, the National Brera Library and the Astronomical Observatory.

The Art Gallery, connected to the Academy, was opened in 1803 and rebuilt between 1946 and 1950, after the heavy bombings of the last war, by the architect Portaluppi under the consultency of the architect Ettore Modigliani.

It includes 38 rooms and gathers more than 500 works of painting and sculpture. Not all of the rooms are always open. To arrive at the Art Gallery one crosses the palace courtyard, with its honor staircase, Richini's masterpiece, at the center of which is found the bronze of Napoleon, modelled after Canova.

From the front atrium one enters directly into a room where the bust of Giovanni Morelli, a bronze by Francesco Barzaghi, and the commemorative stones of Ettore Modigliani and Fernanda Wittgens are kept.

ROOM I. Among the major pictorial works contined in this room: *The Painter's Family* by Francesco Nuvolone; *Self-Portrait* by Palma the Younger; *Self-Portrait* by Giandomenico Ferretti; *Self-Portrait* by Francesco Hayez.

ROOM II. This small room, with its characteristic dimensions, recalls the structure of the oratory of the counts Porro and Mocchirolo, whose frescoes are housed here, donated to the Art Gallery by their owners: the cycle of 14th-century Lombard mastery of the school of Giovanni da Milano.

ROOM III. To note: *Jesus in the garden* by Paolo Veronese, and inportant work of late maturity; *St. Sebastian, Costantine and Helen, Rocco* by Palma the Elder; *Madonna in Glory and Sts. Peter, Dominic, Paul and Jerome* by Gerolamo Salvoldo; *Our Lady of the Assumption with Sts. Jerome, Catherine of Alexandria, and Clair* by Moretto; *Pietà* by Lorenzo Lotto; *Baptism and temptations of Jesus* by Paolo Veronese.

ROOM IV. Here are kept works by 16th-century Venetian painters, including: *Supper in the house of the Pharisee,* by Paolo Veronese;

St. Rocco visits the plague victims by Jacopo Bassano; *Discovery of the body of St. Mark* by Jacopo Tintoretto; *Moses saved by the waters* by Bonifacio Veronese; *St. Mark's Prayer in Alexandria of Egypt* by Gentile and Giovanni Bellini.

ROOM VI. Here we can admire Bramantesque frescoes from the Baron Hall of Palazzo Panigarola. They represent famous men of the times: *The man of arms, The Singer, The man with the sword, The man with the mace, The man with the halberd.*

ROOM VIII. Here are kept paintings from the fourteenth and early fifteenth centuries. Significant: *Stories of St. Columba* by an unknown artist; *St. Verano and episodes from his life* by the Master of San Verano; *Christ the Judge* by Giovanni da Milano; *Coronation of the Virgin and Saints* by Gentile da Fabriano; *Adoration of the Magi* by Stefano D'Azeglio; *Madonna with Child* by Ambrogio Lorenzetti.

ROOM VII AND ROOMS IX THROUGH XVII. Here, works by Lombard and Piedmontese painters from the fifteenth and sixtenth century are displayed, including: in room VII *Triptych of Madonna with Child and Sts. Leonard and Bernardine* by Bernardino Butinone; in XI, *Madonna with Child and the blessed Stefano Marconi* by Bergognone; *Madonna with Child, doctors of th church, Ludovico il Moro, Beatrice*

St. Sebastian, by Vincenzo Foppa.

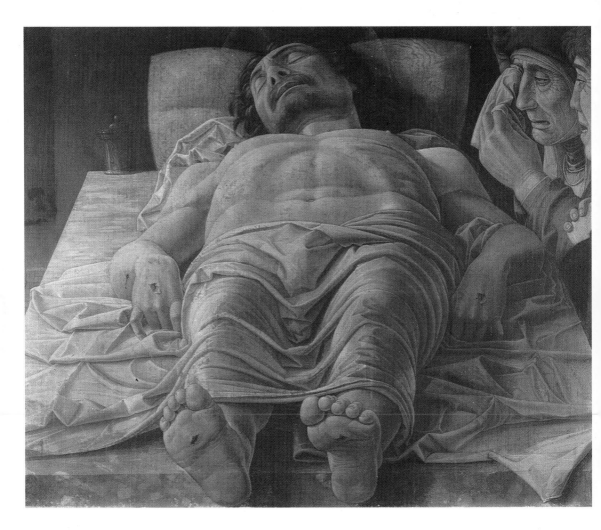

d'Este, by the Master of the Sforza Pala; *Portrait of a Youth* by Ambrogio de Predis; è in XI, *Portrait of a youth by Ambrogio Solario; Madonna with Child and offerer* by Bramantino; in XII, *Madonna with Child* by Cesare de Sesto; in XIV, *St. Andrew and Sts. Catherine and Sebastian* by Martino Spanzotti; *The Archangels Michael, Raphael and Gabriel strike down the demon* by Marco d'Oggioni; *Polyptych with Madonna and Saints* by Vincenzo Foppa, *Crucifixion* by Bramantino.

ROOM XVIII. Hosts works by Andrea Mantegna and Carlo Crivelli, notable among which: *Dead Christ, St. Luke the Evangelist and Saints* by Mantegna; *Crucifixion and Madonna with Candle, Coronation of Mary, Dead Christ and Madonna with Child and Saints* by Crivelli.

Above, the Dead Christ by Mantegna.
On the facing page, Madonna with son and saints by Ercole De Roberti.

paintings: *Madonna with Child, Angels, Saints, and Federico da Montefeltro* by Piero della Francesca, and *Wedding of the Virgin* by Raphael.

The room also hosts the Processional symbol of Santa Maria delle Grazie a Fabriano painted by Luca Signorelli, and the *Madonna of milk*, again by Luca Signorelli.

ROOM XXVII. The most interesting work is *The Madonna with Child and Saints* by Gerolamo Genga, an enormous wooden pala (1513-1518) created for the Church of St. Augustine in Cesena.

ROOM XXVIII. Here we can admire works by Carracci and his followers: *Martyrdom of San Vitale* by Barocci; La Cananea; The Samaritan at the well by Annibale Carracci; *The adulteress*

ROOM XIX. Here we can admire Venetian painters from the fifteenth and sixteenth centuries. To note: *Wedding of the Virgin and Presentation of the Virgin at the Temple* by Vittore Capaccio; two *Madonnas with Child* and one *Pietà* by Giovanni Bellini.

ROOM XX. Hosts Emilian and Venetian painters from the fifteenth and sixteenth centuries. Significant: *Madonna of the cherubs* by Andrea Mantegna; *St. John the Baptist and St. Peter* by Francesco del Cossa; *Adoration of the Magi and Nativity* by Correggio.

ROOM OF PIERO DELLA FRANCESCA AND RAPHAEL. The room is divided into three areas: one for Bramante (ROOM XXIV), one for Piero della Francesca (ROOM XXV), one for Raphael (ROOM XXVI). It holds two famous

Above left: St. Jerome by Tiziano Vecellio.
Facing page: Bramante's Christ at the column.

On the following pages: Holy Conversation by Piero della Francesca; Marriage of the Virgin by Raphael and Supper at Emmaus by Caravaggio.

by Agostino Carracci; *Sts. Peter and Paul* by Guido Reni.

ROOM XXIX. Here are displayed paintings by Caravaggio and his followers: *Supper of Emmaus* by Caravaggio; *The Samaritan at the well* by Battistello Caracciolo; *The martyrs Veriano, Tiburzio and Cecilia* by Orazio Gentileschi.

ROOM XXX. To point out, the *Repudiation of Hagar* by Guelcino.

ROOM XXXI. Significant: *Malta Horseman* by Bernardo Strozzi; *Portrait of a gentlewoman and Madonna with Child and St. Anthony of Padua* by Antonio Van Dyck; *The Last Supper* by Peter Paul Rubens.

ROOM XXXII. The *Triptych* by Jan de Beer is important.

ROOM XXXIII. To note, the portrait of a *Young Woman* by Rembrandt.

ROOM XXXIV. Significant: *Madonna of Carmel* by Giambattista Tiepolo; *Madonna with Child and Saints* by Pietro da Cortona.

ROOMS XXXV and XXXVI. Here we can admire the works of eighteenth-century Italian painters. To note: *View of the Grand Canal* by Francesco Guardi; *View of the Gazzada* by Bellotto; *View of the Grand Canal* by Canaletto; *Rebecca at the well* by Giovanni Battista Piazzetta; *Lord Donoughmore* by Joshua Reynolds; *Portrait of the Singer Domenico Annibali* by Anton Raphael Mengs; *A Fair* by Crespi; *Portaroli* by Giacomo Ceruti.

NEW WING. Reached from ROOM VIII. To note: *Portrait of the painter Moisé Kisling* by Amedeo Modigliani; *The city rising and Fight in a tunnel* by Umberto Boccioni; *Rhythms of Object* by Carlo Carrà; *North/South* by Gino Severini; *The carpenter's bench by Ottone Rosai; The house of love and The marble sawmill* by Carlo Carrà; *Urban Landscape with Trucks* by Mario Sironi; *Marina still life with scampi and Still life with eggs* by Filippo De Pisus. *At the center, three wax figures* by Medardo Rosso, *L'enfant juif, La petite rose and La femme et la voilette;* two terracotta works by Arturo Martini: *The drinker and Ophelia.*

Metaphysical painting is represented by The metaphysical muse, Mother and child, The enchanted room by Carlo Carrà, the Roman school by *Cardinal Vannutelli on his deathbed and Still*

life with sole and coin by Scipione; *Quartered ox and Dried flowers* by Mario Mafai; Long senna of the Invalids; Peonies; San Moisé; Marine still life with pen by Filippo De Pisis.

Futurism is represented by *Elasticity and The drinker* by Umberto Boccioni; *Automobile plus speed plus light rounds, Laughing brush, Patriotic demonstration* by Giacomo Balla; *Nocturne in Piazza Beccaria* by Carlo Carrà; *The bus* by Gino Severini; *Trenches and White Ballerina* by Mario Sironi; *Lines and volumes in a street* by Ardengo Soffici; *Bottle Zag Tumb Tumb* by Ottone Rosai.

Hours: Tuesday through Friday, 9 a.m. - 2 p.m. Saturday: 9 a.m.-1 p.m. *Closed Mondays.*

In the same complex which holds the Art Gallery, there is also the NATIONAL BRERA LIBRARY, second staircase after the corridor. Founded by Maria Theresa of Austria in 1763, it numbers approximately one million titles. Maria Theresa of Austria also founded the *ACADEMY OF FINE ARTS* in 1766 where famous artists still teach. A separate sector is formed by the *ASTRONOMICAL OBSERVATORY.*

The metaphysical muse by Carrà.

ITINERARY Nr. 4:
FROM THE CASTLE
TO SANTA MARIA DELLE GRAZIE

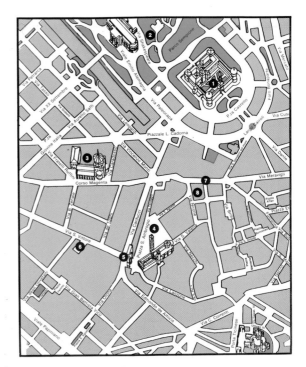

SFORZA CASTLE

History

The Sforza Castle, one of the symbols of Milan, was built between 1358 and 1368 as a bulwark of the western part of Milan, which was left to Galeazzo II Visconti, son of Matteo and brother of Bernabò, who instead inherited the eastern part of the city upon his father's death. A section of the wall with Porta Giovia, from which the castle took its long-ago name, was included in the construction. Gian Galeazzo, son of Galeazzo II, expanded the castle, and his descendants Giovanni Maria and Filippo Maria, in addition to confirming its strategic importance, also chose it as the family residence. The historians Vasari and Baldinucci testify that Filippo Brunelleschi was also called to the Visconti court to give his opinions on the work to be done.

After the fall of the Sforzas during the golden Ambrosian Republic, the Castle was destroyed. It returned upon the arrival of Duke Francesco Sforza, to whom the Castle's current structure is due, who called Giovanni da Milano, Filippo Scorzioli da Ancona and Jacopo da Cortona for the reconstruction designs, as well as Filarete who, however, soon left the job due to conflicts. At the time of Sforza's death in 1466, the works were nearly completed, and his son Galeazzo Maria transferred the ducal residence there, which until then had been in the Royal Palace next to the Duomo. Thereafter the castle became a luxurious residence, and was embellished with many works of art, for whom Vincenzo Foppa, Cristoforo Moretto, Benedetto Ferrini were called; the garden was expanded and new architectural works were done.

The embellishment project was taken up again and continued by Ludovico il Moro, regent for Galeazzo Maria's young son, Gian Galeazzo. Moro also called famous artists to the court, including Bramante and Leonardo da Vinci, who in 1491 directed the wedding of Ludovico and Beatrice d'Este. When, after the death of the last Sforza, the Castle passed into Spanish hands, it lost all connotations as a residence and was fortified as much as possible, becoming one of the best-armed citadels of Europe: bulwarks were added, the moats were completed and the street paved.

The Sforza Castle with the Filarete Tower or Watchtower. Glimpses of the tower, the bridge and the walls of the Sforza Castle.

It remained intact until 1733, when the French troops and the Savoias, commanded by General Villard, massacred the Castle, which gave in after a long siege with Annibale Visconti. With

The Sforza Castle with the Filarete Tower or Watchtower. Glimpses of the tower, the bridge and the walls of the Sforza Castle.

which was lost in 1521 following an explosion of the powder-magazine.

Seventy meters tall and topped by two elevations of decreasing volume, the tower stands over the arched drawbridge gate, now walled up. Two statues on the gate: one dedicated to Umberto I on horseback, by Luigi Secchi in 1916, and above a statue of St. Ambrose. The sides of the building are similar to the main façade in structure and decoration. The Vercellina or Holy Spirit Gate opens on the left side, beyond which one finds the ruins of a ravelin which was once connected to the Ghirlandina enclosure. The right side has a small bridge named after Ludovico il Moro, the work of Bramante but now rebuilt by Beltrami, which was also connected to the Ghirlanda across the moat with two archivolts. On the same side is the Carmini Gate. The rear which faces to Sempione Park, is broken by Porta Barco and flanked by two square towers. Looking at this side from outside the castle, one can see the Castellana tower to the right, the Falconiera tower to the left. Around the castle ran a paved road, a corridor from the counter-cliff of the moat, which connected the castle to the open countryside in ways which have remained partially secret to this day. The generous quadrilateral of the Castle is divided internally into three courtyards.

Napoleon, what remained was transformed and restructured, the monumental Bonaparte Forum — which surrounded all of it with imposing constructions — was designed, and additional transformations took place in the last century. In 1893 the architect Luca Beltrami, after long study, documented reconstructions and deductions, returned the Castle to its fifteenth-century appearance, making it worthy once again of the Sforza name. It was inaugurated in 1904 as we see it today.

The castle today

The imposing square figure of the Castle, which one reaches by travelling along via Orefici and via Dante from Piazza Duomo, covers and area of 40,000 square meters. The main façade, facing largo Cairoli, presents a high embattled curtain and is opened by large biforate windows with terracotta pointed arches. At the sides are the round towers rebuilt by Betrami, the same as in the 1500's, and in the center of the façade stands the tall Filarete Tower or Watchtower, another reconstruction of the ancient tower

Above, the Visconti coat-of-arms with snake symbol. On the facing page, detail of a round tower with the Visconti coat-of-arms, with the slim Watchtower in the background.

Militia Courtyard. Entered from the door of the main façade. On the right there are the remains of old Milanese houses and Roman relics. Across from the entrance is the statue of San Giovanni Nepomuceno, created by Dugnani in 1729 by order of Annibale Visconti.

The rear wall divides the Main Courtyard from the Rocchetta Courtyard and the Ducal Courtyard. In front of the wall is the dead moat, the bed of the Canal which in the fourteenth century surrounded the walls of the city.

Rocchetta Courtyard. A true citadel, the last bulwark in which the Sforza hid in case of danger.

It is lined with porticos, once magnificently decorated and frescoed: to the left, entering from the Militia Cortyard, the portico built by Filarete for Francesco Sforza, in front, the one built by Benedetto Ferrini for Galeazzo Maria; right, the one ordered from Bramante by Ludovico il Moro.

The porticoed building to the left by Filarete housed Ludovico il Moro and Beatrice d'Este before they moved to the Ducal Palace as Lords of Milan, after the death of Gian Galeazzo. In the building in front of the entrance we find the hall of the Ducal Council, where Moro held the solemn meetings of the Council of State. In the hall above, 900 square meters, ball games were played (Sala della Balla).

At the base of the square tower, not visible from inside, was the Sforza's treasure room, with a large fresco by Bramante portraying Argus, which reappeared from under the plaster in 1894. Above the small door which led to the room of the Duke's personal treasure appears the message: *Adulterinae abite claves*, false keys keep away!

Between the Castle and Ducal courtyards stands the austere Tower ordered built by Bona di Savoia, wife of Galeazzo Maria Visconti and mother of Gian Galeazzo, to defend herself from Ludovico il Moro — her son's protector, but whom she apparently did not trust.

Ducal Courtyard. Entered through the Porta Giovia from the Main Courtyard, it is crowned by the Sforza coat-of-arms. After the vestibule one arrives in the most important and meaningful part of the entere castle.

The courtyard was built by Ferrini on order of Galeazzo Maria, and was the residence of the dukes. The building surrounding it has only one storey and two rows of windows with fired-brick pointed arches. In the rear is the Elephant portico, again by Ferrini, also the artist of the two-storey gallery, in the early Renaissance Lombard

style, and of the staircase of Galeazzo Maria.

The Horse staircase also begins in the courtyard, so called because the low, wide steps could be climbed even by their mounts. The right wing is opened by a portal from 1555, ordered by a Spanish governor.

THE CASTLE MUSEUMS

The Sforza Castle is the site of many rich and prestigious museums:

— **Civic collections of ancient art**, including the Sculpture Collection and Picture Gallery;

— **Civic collections of applied art**, with the Museum of musical instruments and the Trivulzio Library;

— **Civic archeological and numismatic collections**, including the collection of Medals, the prehistoric and Egyption sections, the Bertarelli Press collection.

Civic collections of ancient art

Entered from the Main Courtyard through the Locksmiths' Pustern, a consistent remainder of the XIV-century wall of Azzone Visconti which until 1900 was located at the end of via Cesare Correnti.

ROOM I. Opening the collection are pre-Christian and medieval Lombard sculptures. Here one can admire architectural elements of the ancient IV-century basilica of Santa Tecla, the marble head said to be of the *Empress Theodora,* Byzantine art of the VI century, the fragment of an enormous head from the Baptistry of San Giovanni in Florence, a pre-Christian sarcophagus found near Lambrate.

ROOM II. Contains works of Romanesque and Champion art, such as the capitals depicting *Scenes from the life of St. Bartholomew,* including a *Exorcism,* the sarcophagus of Giovanni da Fagnano and that of Vieri da Bassignana, the sepulchral monument of Regina della Scala and that of Bernabò Visconti, earlier located in the apse of San Giovanni in Conca, whose ark is supported by

twelve gold-plated and decorated columns.

ROOM III. This is perhaps the ancient chapel of San Donato, as can be deduced from the decorations on the ceiling. Here we find: a window mandorla with the Redeemer and Our Lady of the Assumption, the sarcophagus of the monk Mirano di Bechaloe, a Campionese work once kept in the cloister of San Marco, statues of the ancient Porta Orientale and Porta Comasina, the tomb slabs of Bianca di Savoia and Antonello Arcimboldi, from the XIV and XV centuries.

ROOM IV. In the vault there is a large coat-of-arms of Philip of Spain and his wife Mary Tundor, works of Campionese art, a tabernacle of the Borgognone school from the XIV century. In a passage leading to ROOM V, a beautiful fire window from the XVI-XVII, depicting among other things the *Judgement of King Solomon..*

ROOM V or CHAPEL ROOM. Contains, among others, the *Headless Madonna* by Giovanni da Balduccio.

ROOM VI or PORTA ROMANA ROOM. Here we find bas-reliefs which once decorated the Porta, and a relief of the Idea procession, later the holiday of Candlemas in Santa Maria Beltrade, now demolished.

ROOM VII or BANNER ROOM. Appropriate to its name, this room holds a city banner from 1566, and on the walls are tapestries of biblicals subjects from the XVII century.

ROOM VIII or BOARD ROOM. Takes its name from the wooden boars which perhaps at one time covered the lower part of the walls and, during Ludovico il Moro's time, it hosted sumptuous receptions. Now it holds the most significant testimony to the many decorations that once adorned the castle: a large painting covering the entire vault and the walls, with a vegetable them, by Leonardo da Vinci.

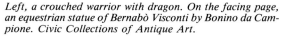

Left, a crouched warrior with dragon. On the facing page, an equestrian statue of Bernabò Visconti by Bonino da Campione. Civic Collections of Antique Art.

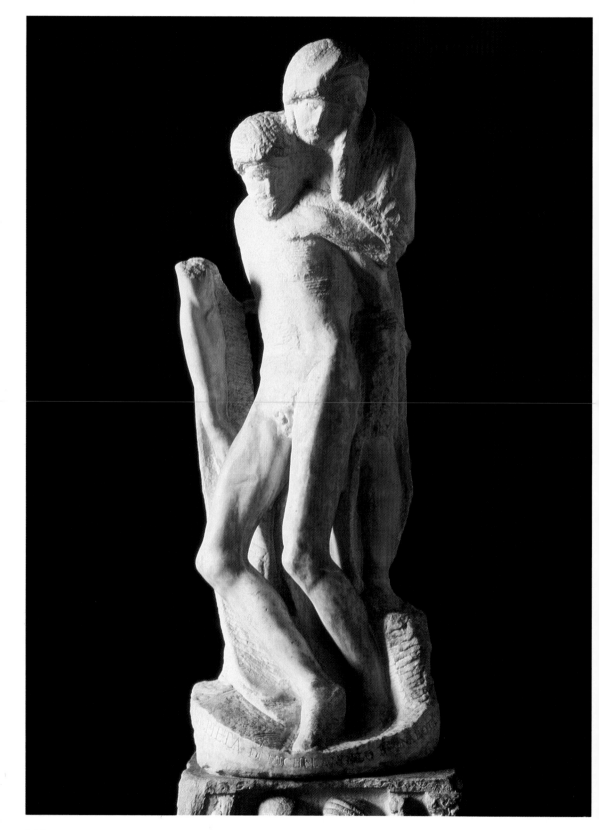

ROOM XI or BLACK ROOM. Here Moro closed himself away in thought after the premature death of Beatrice d'Este.

In the lunettes are *Portraits of the Sforzas*, with the whole dynasty, attributed to Bernardino Luini and once kept in the house of the Atellani family in corso Magenti, and a few tombs.

ROOM X. Holds some portraits of the Sforzas and paintings from the Lombard sixteenth century.

ROOM XI or DUKES' ROOM. Here we find large coats-of-arms of Galeazzo Maria Sforza, important sculptures and a marble slab by the Tuscan Agostino Duccio with *St. Sigismund travelling to the Monastery of Sagauno.*

ROOM XII. Completely frescoed and restored.

On the facing page, the Pietà Rondanini by Michelangelo. Below, the tomb of Gastone di Foix by Bambaia. Civic collections of Antique Art.

ROOM XIII or DOVE ROOM, so named for the doves which Bona di Savoia had painted with the Visconti motto a *bon droit*. Contains important sculptures form the Lombard Renaissance.

ROOM XIV. Contains the Civic arms collection. One enters through two doorways, one from the XV century and one Renaissance.

Here are found the doorways of now-demolished Milanese houses, such as the one in marble from the Medici Bank, in via dei Bossi, by Vasari. The arms collection is divided into white defensive arms and firearms.

ROOM XV, or SCARLIONI ROOM. Hosts the horizontal statue of *Gastone di Foix*, an important work by Bambaia, and in the other room the *Pietà Rondanini* by Michelangelo, a late and incomplete work by the master, designed in 1552 and returned to in 1555. At the exit, the only authentic window of the castle, in fired brick, which Luca Beltrami used as a reference for the reconstruction.

ROOM XVI. Holds the Furniture Collection, with pieces from the XV to the XVIII centuries, mostly from nothern Italy, begun with the purchase of the Mora Collection.

Extremely precious are the wooden chair known as "il corretto" by Torrechiara, a Lombard trunk, a sacristy bench, and a Tyrol cupboard from 1630 with 21 carved drawers.

ROOM XVII or GRISELDA ROOM. So named for the cycle of frescoes which narrate the story of Boccaccio's Griselda. Here valuable furniture is also kept, including a trunk decorated with three coat-of-arms medallions, wooden sculptures, ad a round table.

ROOMS XVIII and XIX. These hold the Art Gallery. Among the most outstanding works: *Polyptych* by Bembo, 1462; *Madonna in glory and saints,* by Mantegna, 1497; *Resurrection* by Lorenzo Veneziano, from 1371; *Madonna with child and Poet Laureate* by Giovanni Bellini; *Portrait of a Youth* by Lotto, *Martyrdom of St. Sebastian* by Vincenzo Foppa, ca. 1480; *Polyptych,* the last work by Cesare da Sesto, from 1523; *Springtime*, in the Arcimboldi style; *Portrait of Henrietta of France* by Van Dyck.

ROOM XXV is used for rotating works of art, and in room XXVI, paintings from the Lombard 17th and 18th centuries.

Above, the polyptych of Torchiara by Benedetto Bembo. Facing page, Madonna in glory among saints and angels by Mantegna. Art Gallery.

On the facing page, Springtime in the style of Arcimboldi. Art Gallery.
Above, the travels of John Mandeville (XV cent.). Trivulziana.

Civic collections of applied art

Located on the top floor of the Castle. They gather statues, ceramics — especially rare and precious Chinese works — majolicas from Faenza, Urbino, Savona and Albisola, Angarano,

Abruzzo castles and Milan. Thery are followed by the porcelain works including some by Sèvres, works in gold, crystal, ivory, and enamel, technical and scientific instruments. Two rooms on the lower floor hold fabrics and work of gold.

Around the Castle Courtyard, the rooms of the Museum of Musical Intruments, which also holds items by Stradivarius and other rare and valuable works. The ''Sala della Balla''.

The Trivulzio Library, still in the Castle, contains precious miniatures, editions from the 15th century and later, for a total of 68,000 volumes, 1,455 cradle books and 1445 miscellaneous.

Above, a manuscript by Bona and Galeazzo Maria Sforza; left and on the facing page, two illustrations of 15th-century texts. Trivulziana.

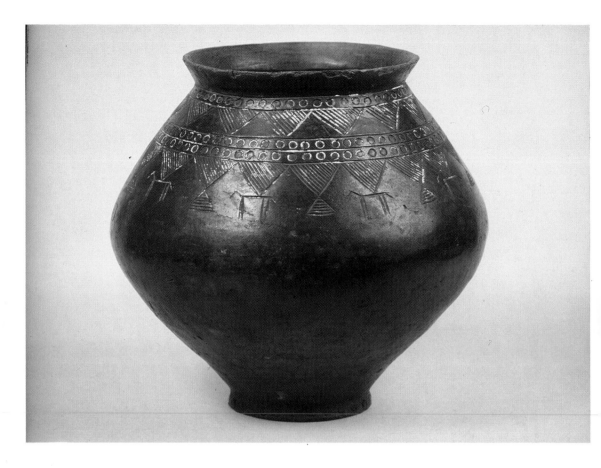

Civic archeological and numismatic collections

Located in the underground vaults of the Castle Courtyard. In the pre-historic section, the evolutionary history of the human race through cranial casts and a signficant collection of arms, tools, magical-religious objects, ceramics, bronzes. A tomb from 2,500 B.C. found in Fontanella di Casalmorano, with the deceased mummified in a flexed position holding a flint knife blade, relics of the Torrazza in Vigevano and of the Cascina Ranza near Milan; accessories from the carriage tomb of Sesto Calende.

The Egyptian section is also interesting, with sarcophagi, a human mummy and scrolls, the important Paeftauauiiset funeral complex, with mummy, double-opening sarcophagus in a human form and the outer case. Also, fragments of the *Book of the Dead*, canopic vases, earthenware, and the seated statue of the Pharaoh Amenemhet III, of exceptional interest.

In the tower by Filarete one can visit the Medal Collection, which gathers coins and medals from various countries and periods, and the Achille Bertarelle Print Collection, which gathers together approximately 600,000 pieces including volumes and single prints.

Hours for all Castle Museums: 9:30 a.m. - 12:15 p.m. /2:30-5:30 p.m. *Archeological Museum closed Tuesdays, others closed Mondays.*

Above, an urn found at Golasecca. On the facing page, above, an Albate vase with ducks; below, Roman glass. Civic Archeological and Numismatic Collections.

SEMPIONE PARK, ARENA, AC-QUARIUM, PALAZZO DELL'ARTE, ARCO DELLA PACE

Through the Gate of the Sforza Castle Park one enters SEMPIONE PARK, which covers a surface area of 47 hectares, not much compared to what was supposed to be the great Ducal park, reserved for the amusement and hunting rounds of the Viscontis and Sforzas, and which also included a lodge, barricades, stock farms, vegetable gardens and orchards.

It now occupies the area where the old Piazza d'Armi was.

Its appearance today is the late-19th century work of Emilio Alemagna, who arranged the vast area between the Castle and the Arc della Pace. Gothic-Lombard style along with the adjacent Dominican convent.

Within the park we find the ACQUARIUM, built by the architect Sebastiano Locati in Liberty style on the occasion of the 1906 International Exposition, and was rebuilt after bombings.

The CIVIC ARENA is also in the Park area: it was constructed in 1808 by Luigi Canonica, who used part of the material from the demolished Sforza Castle. It is an amphitheatre in an elliptical shape, 238 by 116 meters, and can hold 30,000 spectators.

Four doors open from the outside wall: to the SE the Porta Trionfale, to the NE Porta Libitinaria, from which the dying gladiators were taken out in the Roman amphitheaters, to the SW the Loggia Reale and to the NW the Porta delle Carceri.

Grandiose shows were held here during the Cisalpine Republic and the Italian Kingdom, when it was also used as a naumachia by filling the interior with water from the Canals.

Replaced for soccer games by the San Siro stadium, today races, shows, and concerts are held here.

Still in the park we find the PALAZZO DELL'ARTE, entered from viale Alemagna. It is a severe and majestic building, marked by large white arcades by the architect Giovanni Muzio in 1931, donated by senator Antonio Bernocchi to the City of Milan. It is the permanent site of the Triennial Exhibition.

The Park Tower is also found in the Park, built in 1933 by Giò Ponti, Chiodi and Ferrari, 108 meters high — like the Madonna on the Duomo, but topped instead by the television station installed on its roof. After a fire which damaged its structure, its future is now uncertain.

On the side opposite the Castle, the Park is bordered by the ARCO DELLA PACE, built according to an original design by Luigi Cagnola in 1807, inspired by the arch with three supporting vaults by Settimo Severo in Rome.

It is made of Baveno granite, covered with marble from Crevola d'Ossola and is topped by the colossal Sestiga della Pace by Abbondio Sangiorgio. Under the trabeation, the four rivers of Lombardy-Venetia are represented: Po, Ticino, Adige and Tagliamento. The name commemorates the European peace treaty of 1815.

Facing page, the Sempione Park.
Above, the Arena; above right, the Acquarium; below, the
Modern Art Building.

125

The Arco della Pace: overall view and details.

CHURCH OF SANTA MARIA DELLE GRAZIE

Located in the square of the same name, which opens onto corso Magenta, it was built in 1463 next to a chapel dedicated to Our Lady of Grace by the will of the Dominican monks, who had received the land as a gift from Gaspare Vimercati, commander of the Sforza militia. The initial project was assigned to Guiniforte Solari, who built it in a holds the fantastic tapestries representing the months, designed by Bramantino.

In 1492 Ludovico il Moro wanted to re-do the tribune, including the cupola and the presbytery, and hired the most renowned artists of the time, including Bramante. On March 29, 1492 the archbishop Guido Antonio Arcimboldi laid the cornerstone of the new tribune, and in 1497 Moro's wife, Beatrice d'Este, was buried there. It was not touched during the Baroque and neoclassical periods, but suffered the pillages of the French under Napoleon. In '43 it was heavily damaged by the bombings.

The interventions by Solario and Bramante are easily visible from the outside. The brick façade is by Solario, marked with ocula and interrupted by the lovely Bramantesque portal covered by the canopy and flanked by pointed-arch windows. The rear wall is made up of the imposing Renaissance tribune with three apses decorated ith pilasters, candelabra, rounds and medallions and covered by the precious polygonal lantern, slimmed by the architraved biforis, which ends in the smaller lantern.

The interior has three naves, separated by serizzo columns which support the arched ogives, from which the ribbed vaults rise up, splendidly decorated with motifs which, hidden in the 1600's, re-appeared during the restorations completed in the nineteenth and twentieth centuries.

The large lunettes over the central nave are the work of Bernardino Butinone, Bernardino Zenale and Montorfano. The naves have six chapels each and contain notable works of art. Here we can admire frescoes by Gaudenzio Ferrari, Giovanni da Schio, the fresco of the *Holy Family with St. Catherine of Alexandria* by Paris Bondone, sculptures by Bambaia. The large tribune has circular arches decorated with radiating wheels and a tambour opened by elegant biforis. The presbytery is embellished by an umbrella vault and receives light from the ocula in the lunettes. In the back of the right nave, one enters the original nucleus of the church, the chapel of

The church of Santa Maria delle Grazie: overall view and details.

the Madonna delle Grazie. The altar is decorated with a pre-Leonardesque panel depicting its donor *Gaspare Vimercati with his family*, protected by the Virgin's mantle; in a lunette of the last bay there is a large canvas by Cerano. Following the bombings, a fresco of the Lombard school from the second half of the XV century re-appeared, portraying the *Holy Father with angel musicians*.

Passing through the new sacristy one exits into the Bramantesque cloister, square with the five bays on each side, which bears frescoes by Bramantino depicting *St. Peter Martyr and St.*

Catherine of Siena. One then enters the old sacristy, finished in 1499, with lovely 15th-century frescoes, and works by Gaudenzio Ferrari and Montalto.

Leaving the church, to the left one enters the refectory which holds one of the worlds artistic masterpieces, LEONARDO DA VINCI'S LAST SUPPER. The large fresco, measuring 9 by 4.5 meters, was ordered from Leonardo da Vinci by Ludovico il Moro in 1495. It required two years of work, during which the artist dedicated himself to days of great fervor alternating with days of deep meditation.

The Last Supper by Leonardo da Vinci at Santa Maria della Grazie.

Unfortunately, the experimental painting techniques used by Leonardo condemned the work right from the start, and it began to deteriorate almost immediately. Rather than oils, Leonardo used materials such as strong tempera, with mixes of lacquer and turpentine, isinglass and resin on two layers of plaster. Already in the late 1500's Paolo Moriggia described it as mostly lost, and in the 1600's Federico Borromeo ordered a copy by Vespino, now in the Ambrosian Art Gallery, to have a testimony of the painting which was inexorably falling to ruin. There have been many attempts at restoration, and the fresco

underwent a radical cleaning in 1953 by Mauro Pelliccioli, but the climate — and especially smog — make it increasingly difficult to preserve the masterpiece.

Details of the Last Supper.

The painting shows the *Last Supper* before the passion, with Christ among his disciples, in the moment in which he is announcing that one of them will betray him. On each face is captured the emotion generated by the announcement.

The figures of the apostles are, from left: Bartholomew, Jacob the Younger, Andrew, Judas, Peter, John and, after Christ, Thomas, Jacob the Elder, Philip, Thaddeus Judas, Simon the Zealot.

The study of the perspective is also quite particular, in which the space between the mensa and the rear wall is identical to half of the actual refectory.

Details of the Last Supper.

Last Supper Hours: Tuesday through Saturday 9 a.m. - 1:30 p.m. */2-6:30 p.m. Sunday and Monday:* 9 a.m. - 1:30 p.m.

BASILICA OF SANT'AMBROGIO

Located in the square of the same name, it is one of the city's oldest and most fascinating basilicas. It was built in 379 on the spot where the saints Gervasio and Protasio were buried, near a Christian cemetery in which the sepulchral chapels of the saints Victor, Naborre, Felice, Vitale and Valeria were to be found. In 397 Ambrose was buried here. It was already a very important basilica, because during the High Middle Ages archbishops were consecrated and Emperors and Kings of Italy were crowned there. In the VII century the complex was passed to the Benedictine monks, who quite soon entered into conflict with the canons of Sant'Ambrogio, although they had originally come to support the latter in the work of the diocese. In the next century, the archbishops Angilberto and Ansperto began the trasformations which will give the basilica its medieval appearance. The apse was changed, the canopy and the monks' bell tower were built, to which the canons replied two centuries later with another bell tower. After it collapsed in 1196, more changes were made to the vault and the lantern was rebuilt, then re-done again by Pellegrini in 1572 on

Two views of the Basilica of Sant'Ambrogio.

order of cardinal Borromeo. Bramante designed the Presbytery at the end of the XV century, ordered by Ludovico il Moro. Baroque retouches were avoided, but the basilica underwent a number of other changes, including those intended to return it to its original appearance. After the bombings in '43 it was rebuilt by Reggiori as we see it today.

Before arriving at the basilica one crosses the atrium, ordered built by the bishop Ansperto in the XI century; porticoed on three sides, it is in the style of the two previous buildings, one from the High Middle Ages and one pre-Christian. To the right, just after the entrance, is the "devil's column", which popular tradition claims was disfigured by Satan himself chased out by Ambrose. Beneath the portico are pre-Christian remains, stones, remains of frescoes, coats-of-arms and heraldic studies of old Milanese patrician families, the ark of Ansperto, Uberto Decembrio's tombstone and the sepulchre of his son Piet Candido Decembrio, humanist and biographer of Filippo Maria Visconti.

The façade has two galleries, one over the other: the lower one with three portals, in the center of which stands the pre-Romanesque sculpture of Ambrose; the upper one has a portico with five sloping arches connected to the women's gallery which lights the interior.

The interior has three naves, the middle one divided into four bays. In the second bay on the left there is a column with a snake, donated by

the Oriental Emperor Basil II to the archbishop Arnolfo II, which according to legend is destined to move during the Apocalypse. On that side is another column base originally from the IV century. Still on the left, beneath the decorated pulpit supported by nine small columns is the pre-Christian sarcophagus by Stilicone, actually the tomb of the emperor Gratianus who died in 383. The presbytery, created in Romanesque times but later rebuilt, is covered by the lantern, rebuilt after the 1196 collapse, and holds the XI-century canopy with its baldachin decorated with colorful stucco work. Beneath the canopy, a masterpiece of the Carolingian goldsmith's art: the golden altar, or frontal, built by the master Volvinio and artists of his school, donated to the basilica by Angilberto II in 836: it is a large wooden case, laminated in gold and silver, studded with gems, pearls and cameos, engraved and cantilevered, stored in a crystal urn. The side which is surely to be attributed to Volvinio, and thus more artistically interesting, is the rear one in gilded silver foil. Here St. Augustine is depicted crowning Angilberto on one side and the artist himself on another. The entrance to the apse is flanked by pilasters whose lower parts date back to the primitive basilica. The apsidal concha is decorated with magnificent frescoes on a gold background, the oldest of which date to the IV century. Here we also find what remains of the VIII-century choir stalls of carved wood, at the center of which

stands the bishops' marble chair, which Ambrose sat upon in the IV century and which, according to tradition, Milanese women used as a birthing chair.

The crypt beneath the apse, entered from the sides of the presbytery, was remade in the XVIII century, but originates in the 10th C. It holds the remains of Ambrose, Gervasius and Protasius, found in the porphyry tomb also located in the crypt, and in the 1800's deposited in the finely decorated silver and crystal urn. The naves of the church above contain precious works of art. In the first chapel on the right are frescoes by Gaudenzio Ferrari, in the second two more of his works at the altar and, on the walls, the *Martyrdom of St. Victor* and *Drowning of San Satiro* by Tiepolo, and frescoes by Luini in the vault. The third chapel is the re-created work of Cagnola and contains the sarcophagus of Marcellina, Ambrose's sister. In the sixth chapel, frescoes by Lanino. After the seventh chapel on the right, through the antechapel of San Satiro, one enters the sacellum of San Vittore in Ciel d'Oro, erected in the IV century where the cemetery of Christian martyrs once stood. Of this apsidal aula, from the pre-Christian era, remains the apse with its small cupola, covered with beautiful V-century mosaics, including the oldest and most realistic portrait of St. Ambrose. In the crypt below are the remains of the tombs of St. Victor and San Satiro.

In the left nave, in the first chapel, a fresco by Bergognone of 1491, and at the end of the nave the sepulchral stone of Pipino, son of Charlemagne and king of Italy, buried in Sant'Ambrogio with two other Carolingian kings: Bernard, ordered blinded by Ludovic the Pious, and Ludovic II. The portico of the presbytery which flanks the left nave was rebuilt after 1943, following the design which Ludovico il Moro had commissioned from Bramante.

Left, Madonna with child and saints by Gaudenzio Ferrari. On the facing page, the sarcophagus of Stilicone, at Sant'Ambrogio.

POSTERN OF SANT'AMBROGIO

Located in front of Sant'Ambrogio, reconstructed, it is the only remainder of the twelve or thirteen "posterns" or minor gates in the medieval walls. It has two barrel vaults and two square towers at its sides. A gothic tabernacle depicting the Saints Ambrose, Bervaso and Protasio, is on the front. Today it houses a Museum of Antique Arms.

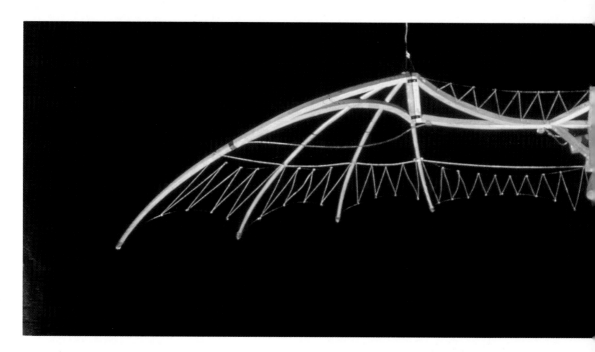

MUSEUM OF SCIENCE AND TECHNOLOGY

This is located in the ex-convent of San Vittore, and entered from via San Vittore nr. 21. The idea of a museum to document human progress in the field of science and technology dates back to the early twentieth century, but it was not created until 1953, the year in which the 500th anniversary of the birth of Leonardo da Vinci was celebrated.

In the left vestibule is a fresco depicting the *Madonna with Child and Saints* by an unknown Lombard artist in the second half of the 1400's. Next, on the right, is an atrium in which a large generator from 1895 is kept. On the right side of the atrium is the exit towards the cloister, whose grassy court is crossed diagonally by the foundation of a fortified enclosure which once enclosed the imperial mausoleum. Next is the cloister, along the back side of which runs the corridor of the textile industry section. Nearby is the *Last Supper Room,* now used for seminars and once the monks' refectory, covered by a lunette vault and adorned by a rich painting.

Along the lower part of the walls is an 18th-century walnut headboard, and in the back a tribune from a Bolognese chancel of the 1700's; against the wall is a small reading pulpit.

Returning towards the entrance atrium, on the left a corridor leads to the cinema room and the bar. Beyond is the entrance to the Civic Museum of Naval Didactics. At the end of the court-

yard is the stair which leads down to the basement room where the sections on metallurgy and foundry work, early motors, land transportation, and petroleum research are hosted.

In the cellar, a hydraulic maul from 1740 for the production of agricultural tools. The E.G. Falck room reproduces a rolling mill from 1862 for drawing metal wire, powered by a 1912 hydraulic turbine. At the back of the room, a nailery from the early 20th century; a lighted panel and model along the wall show a modern Falck rolling mill.

In the basement gallery the historical evolution of metallurgy and foundry is documented. The two reconstructed areas are interesting: the first is a bell foundry (late XVII-early XVIII centuryes), the second a steel and cast iron foundry (late XIX-early XX centuries). Through the door is the section on non-ferrous metals. In the section on petroleum research, processes of mineral formation, original mining tools, fossils attesting to the formation of coal, and the various extraction and refining techniques for petroleum are documented. At the end of the gallery are a few tombs.

The section on land transport documents, with materials from every period, the historical process of means of land transport, from the Hur

The Flying Man by Leonardo da Vinci, at the Museum of Science and Technology.

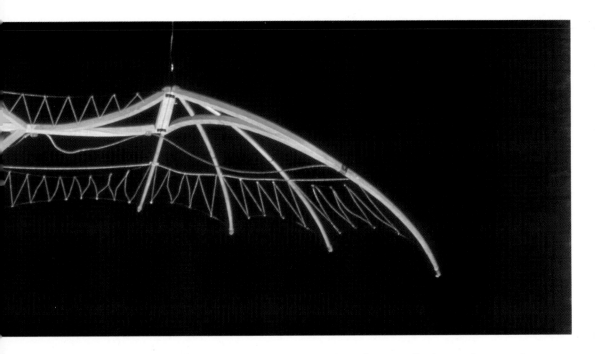

wheel (4,000 B.C.) to modern tires. The section on photography and cinema begins from the first floor landing. To the side is the graphic arts section, which documents the evolution of writing and in which we find paper-making machines and tools. A goldsmith's shop has also been reconstructed. One then arrives at the Leonardo da Vinci Gallery, which constitutes a rich documentation of Leonardo's works. The informatics section is arranged in the parallel room to the left. Perpendicular to the Leonardo Gallery is the section on time measurement, with numerous examples of clocks, from the most ancient solar types to those using sand and water.

The acoustics section contains the first models of phonographs. The reconstruction of a lute-maker's shop precedes the section on musical instruments.

The Leonardo Gallery is divided into two sectors by a high vault, the walls of which are decorated with detached frescoes by Bernardino Luini (*Madonna with Child and Saints Anthony Abbot and Barbara, Madonna which Child and St. John; Angel musicians*).

Returning to the Leonardo Gallery one moves into the second section, flanked by rooms and galleries rotating around the second cloister. On the left, parallel to the gallery, are the sections on modern physics and instrumentation.

At the back of the Leonardo Gallery can the noted several detached frescoes. To the right are the rooms dedicated to astronomy, telecommunications, optics and electrology. In a raised passage, there is a small planetarium set for command lighting. A Foucault pendulum demonstrates the Earth's rotation.

Following the left side of the astronomy section is the part dedicated to radio and television. In the Guglielmo Marconi Room can be found original curios and a model of the yacht "Elettra". At the end of the room are two other sections of the museum dedicated to optics and electrology. In the rear is a model of the Cern synchroton (particle accelerator).

From the land transport section, one arrives outside to the railway transport section. A drilling tower for petroleum research, 35 meters high, is installed in one corner of the courtyard.

The air and naval transport sections are divided into two areas: to the upper floor is the aeronautics section, and on the lower floor the section on naval transport.

In the basement, within the areas on agriculture and food, various machines for working the land can be seen: seeders, threshers and tractors.

The Civic Didactic Museum and the Cormio Wood Specimen Collection are also located in the monastery. The Naval Museum, which numbers nearly four thousand recorded pieces, represents one of the most consistent Italian collections in the didactical field of naval constructions. In one building of the external court and a basement annex is arranged the Cormio Civic Wood Specimen Collection, which gathers more than seven thousand samples of wood.

141

CHURCH OF SAN MAURIZIO AT THE MAIN MONASTERY

Located at the corner of corso Magenta and via Luini, this is the church of the destroyed Benedictine monastery, the Main Monastery, which according to tradition was founded by Queen Theololinda in the VII century.

The church is the Renaissance creation of Giovanni Giacomo Dolcebuono, who built it in 1503. It gathers a number of works by Bernardino Luini, commissioned by Alessandro Bentivoglio when his daughter entered the convent and when his sons Gian Pietro and Aurelio entered the priesthood. Significant, among others, are those in the choir loft: *Busts of Female Saints, Herodias with the head of the Baptist, Stories of the Passion, Departure to Calvary and the Taking Down from the Cross.* There is also a wooden body, again by Dolcebuono.

The bell tower of the church consists of a square tower, the foundation of which is the remains of the prisons of the Roman circus which extended between corso Magenta and the Crossroads.

CIVIC ARCHEOLOGICAL MUSEUM

At nr. 15 of corso Magenta, in the courtyards of the ex-Benedictine monastery, stands the Civic Archeological Museum.

At the center of the cloister is an engraved stone from Val Canonica, dating from the end of the III or beginning of the II millenium, the Bronze Age.

In the rooms, a vast collection of artifacts from republican and imperial Milan, Greek and Roman artifacts, sarcophagi, glass, ceramics and the famous patera of Parabiago from the IV century A.D., a plate in gilded silver with engravings of the goddess Cybèle. In an inner courtyard can be seen the polygonal tower o the Maximilian walls, known as Ansperto, later incorporated into the wall in the IX century.

Hours: 9:30 a.m. - 12:15 p.m. /2:30-5:30 p.m. Closed Tuesdays.

Top left and right, interior and exterior photos of the Church of San Maurizio.
Bottom left and right, the Archeological Museum and the polygonal tower of Maximilian.

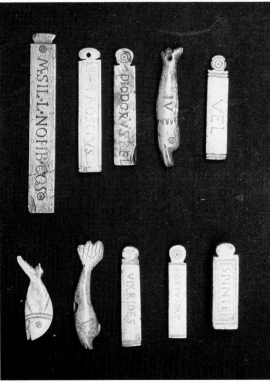

Top left, Greek hydria with chariot scenes; right, an attic crater with banquet scenes; bottom left, ivory Roman theatre passes.
Facing page, top: silver pantera from Parabiago with scenes of the Cybele cult (III cent. A.D.); bottom, silver plate called the «Fisherman's Plate» (III cent. A.D.). Archeological Muse-ʼum.

ITINERARY Nr. 5:
SAN SIRO AND THE CARTHUSIAN MONASTERIES

1 - **San Siro Stadium**, *via Piccolomini nr. 5;*
2 - **Trotter**, *via Piccolomini nr. 1;* 3 - **Hippo-drome**, *piazzale dello sport;* 4 - **Lido**, *piazzale Lotto;* 5 - **Carthusian Monastery of Gareg-nano**, *via Certosa di Garegnano;* 6 - **Chia-ravalle Abbey**, *Chiaravalle;* 7 - **Viboldone Abbey**, *Viboldone, San Giuliano Milanese;*
8 - **Mirasole Abbey**, *City of Opera.*

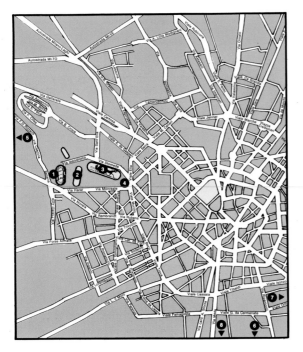

SAN SIRO, TROTTER, HIPPODROME, LIDO

The large sports facilities are grouped together in the area north-west of Milan.

SAN SIRO STADIUM. Located in via Pic-colomini nr. 5, it was built in '26 as the official field of the Milan team, and rebuilt in '55. Since '80 it has become the Giuseppe Meazza stadium and can hold 80,000 spectators.

Still in via Piccolomini, at nr. 1, the TROT-TER of San Siro, with a 1-km track in which approximately 200 races are held each year. Built in '25, it was restructured after the war and raised to the highest European standards.

For gallop and obstacle races, there is the HIPPODROME, in piazzale dello Sport. Built in '21, it covers an area of 600,000 square meters, with stables, chalets, and training gardens.

The largest swimming pool in Milan, the LIDO, is found in piazzale Lotto. When inaugurated in 1930 it was the largest complex in Europe, with 1,200 square meters of water surface divided between two large pools. It also holds other entertainment facilities such as tennis and bocce courts.

Two views of the San Siro Stadium.

CARTHUSIAN MONASTERY
OF GAREGNANO

Located on the street of the same name, to the right of viale Certosa, it dates to 1349, when it was founded on the orders of archbishop Giovanni Visconti. The Carthusian monastery was expanded and restructured at the end of the 1500's, perhaps by Pellegrino Tibaldi; of the old complex, only a few traces remain, towards the highway.

The annexed church of Santa Maria Assunta was re-worked in late-Renaissance form and is the work of Galeazzo Alessi and Vincenzo Seregni, but was completed in the early 17th century. The three-rowed façade is richly decorated with architectural motifs.

The interior holds a fresco decoration, a mesterpiece by the painter Daniele Crespi, who perhaps sought refuge here after committing murder. Here the great painter worked in the early 1600's on the *History of the foundation of the Carthusian Order by St. Bruno*, the theme of the frescoes.

The Carthusian monastery had illustrious guests: Francesco Petrarca in the summer of 1357, followed by St. Bernardine of Siena and Philip IV of Spain.

Two views of the Garegnano Monastery: cloister and façade.

CHIARAVALLE ABBEY

Located in the south-eastern area of Milan, the original nucleus was founded in 1135 by the Cistercian Bernardo di Clairvaux, from whom its name is derived. The monks, skilled and expert farmers, transformed the land donated by Milanese patricians — which consisted of a vast marshy area — into fertile irrigated meadows with rich crops.

The old abbey was replaced as early as 1150 by a new construction and was consecrated in 1221. In about 1347 the octagonal lantern by Francesco Pecorari was topped by the very tall and lovely tower, which reflected the Cistercians' style according to which anything superfluous,

such as isolated bell towers, should be eliminated.

In the Bramante era, and uncertainly attributed to Bramante himself, the large cloister and chapter-house were built. The monastery's agony began with the Spaniards; it died completely and was destroyed during the Cisalpine Republic.

The restorations, begun by Luca Beltrami in 1894, were continued in 1905 by Gaetano Moretti, ad finally completed in 1958 by Reggiori, after the monks had returned there in 1951.

The solemn interior, in Latin cross form, contins 16th- and 17th-century works by Luini, the Campi brothers, and the Fiammenghinis and a splendid wooden choir stall from the mid-17th century, the work of the great wood-carver Carlo Garavaglia. Legend has it that he had sought refuge

among the Cistercians after committing fratricide, became a monk and carved his work as atonement.

The outside cemetery recounts years of Lombard history. Here were buried Pagano, Jacopo, Martino and Filippo Torriani, Ottone Visconti, the Archinto and Piolas families. Of these burials remain only the traces of frescoes, coats-of-arms and stones (in the church). Even Guglielmina Boema, who died in 1241 with an air of sanctity and was worshipped as the Incarnation of the Woman of the Lord, was buried here. After her death she was judged a heretic and her bones were disinterred and scattered, while here followers were burned in piazza Vetra.

The Chiaravalle Abbey with a detail of the bell tower.

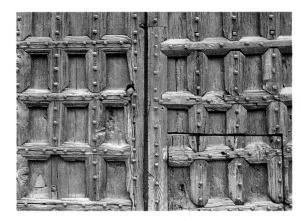

VIBOLDONE ABBEY

Located in the town of the same name, a fraction of San Giuliano Milanese. It was founded in the XIII century by the Humiliati order, created the previous century by Pope Innocent II, which included lay communities of proletarians and craftsmen and religious communities, and who also settled at Mirasole. The order was suppressed in 1571 by Pope Pius V. The Olivetans settled here afterwards.

After being destroyed and then rebuilt after the war, it is currently inhabited by Benedictine monks.

The church, the only building — although restored — of the original complex, was begun in 1176, and its Romanesque and Gothic-Lombard style façade was completed in the XIV century. In the façade, with its sloping architectural style, the mixed features of Romanesque and Gothic-Lombard styles are evident in the prevalent use of brickwork, with a division into three parts by round pilaster strips and lateral reinforcements, with open monoforis and biforis on the sides. The large oculum and the stone portal opening into the façade accentuate the combination of widely different materials such as brick and stone.

In the lunette of the portal and in the two aediculare on the sides, statues depicting the *Madonna with Child and Saints* are visible, the work of an anonyumous Campionese sculptor called the Master of Viboldone.

Behind the church, the lovely bell tower rises towards the sky, opened with monoforis and crowned by a conical cuspid.

The interior has three naves, divided by pointed arches on thick cylindrical pilasters and covered by strong cross-vaults.

The church, once completely covered with admirable frescoes on the interior, now holds, in the last bay of its back wall, the fresco paintings *Madonna on the throne and Saints*, by an unknown Florentine master, a student of Giotto, and *Last Judgement*, perhaps the work of Giusto de' Menabuoni, which stands out for the brilliance of its colors and its grandiose style.

Facing page, details of the façade of the Viboldone Abbey. On this and following pages, Giottesque frescoes and the inner naves.

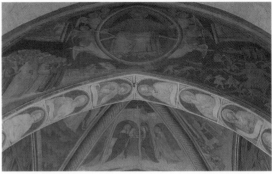

MIRASOLE ABBEY

Located at the gates of Milan, in the town of Opera.

Like the Viboldone Abbey, it was founded by the Humiliati in the XIII century, and after 1797 was granted to the Main Hospital of Milan, its current owner, who has followed and financed its restoration in recent years.

The current structure is, overall, the same as the original, and the restorations have made it possible to use the building once again. It is destined to house the archives and library of Ca' Granda.

On the facing page, an interior view of the Viboldone Abbey. This page, the Mirasole Abbey complex and a detail of the bell tower.

MILAN

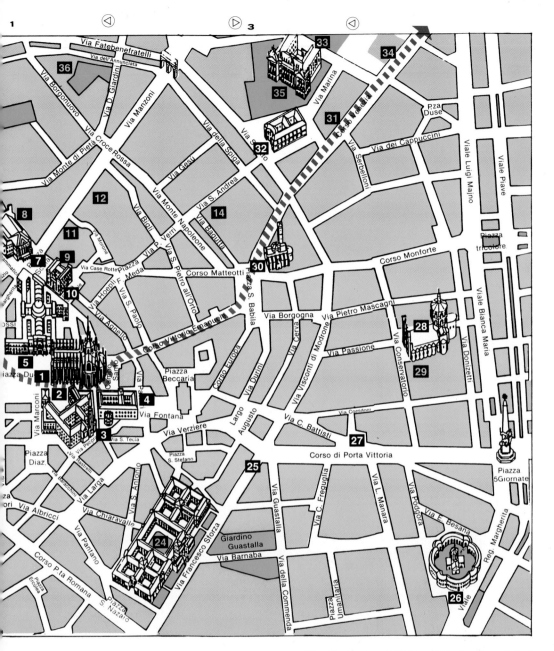

INDICE

Publisher ITALCARDS bologna - italy

Printed at the
Fotometalgrafica Emiliana printing press.
San Lazzaro di Savena - Bologna